Air Fryer Cookbook

for Beginners

500 Instant, Healthy, Delicious Recipes

To Fry, Roast, Grill and Bake.

Written By

Jennifer Newman

Legal & Disclaimer

The information contained in this book and its contents is not designed to replace or take the place of any form of medical or professional advice; and is not meant to replace the need for independent medical, financial, legal or other professional advice or services, as may be required. The content and information in this book has been provided for educational and entertainment purposes only.

The content and information contained in this book has been compiled from sources deemed reliable, and it is accurate to the best of the Author's knowledge, information and belief. However, the Author cannot guarantee its accuracy and validity and cannot be held liable for any errors and/or omissions. Further, changes are periodically made to this book as and when needed. Where appropriate and/or necessary, you must consult a professional (including but not limited to your doctor, attorney, financial advisor or such other professional advisor) before using any of the suggested remedies, techniques, or information in this book.

Upon using the contents and information contained in this book, you agree to hold harmless the Author from and against any damages, costs, and expenses, including any legal fees potentially resulting from the application of any of the information provided by this book. This disclaimer applies to any loss, damages or injury caused by the use and application, whether directly or indirectly, of any advice or information presented, whether for breach of contract, tort, negligence, personal injury, criminal intent, or under any other cause of action.

You agree to accept all risks of using the information presented inside this book.

You agree that by continuing to read this book, where appropriate and/or necessary, you shall consult a professional (including but not limited to your doctor, attorney, or financial advisor or such other advisor as needed) before using any of the suggested remedies, techniques, or information in this book.

Table of Contents

Chapter 4 95

Chapter 5 117

Chapter 6 126

Chapter 7........................164

Dinner Recipes 164

Conclusion.................... 190

Introduction

An Air Fryer is an appliance that mainly uses a hot air system distributed through fans to cook food. This is how the air fryer works; although it depends on the model, it may vary slightly.

Oil-free fryers help you prepare food more healthily thanks to the fact that they fry through hot air. In a way, these fryers are similar to a miniature oven, cooking food with lots of hot air circulating at high speed. These fryers are known in two forms, oilless fryers or air fryers.

Perhaps you may come to think that oil-free fryers are similar and straightforward devices among all the models that exist. However, when you go to buy an oil-free fryer, it is essential that you take into account some aspects, which differentiate an oil-free fryer from another to make it easier for you to choose the fryer that best suits your needs.

There many benefits when using an air fryer. They are easy to use and clean. They do not cause odor because the air or steam they expel is infinitely less than that of conventional fryers, and of course, the lower consumption of fat and cholesterol in the food must be noted.

In this book, you will find many aspects to consider when it comes to an air fryer. Also, we are going to give you the best tips to choose the best air fryer. And finally, you will find information to clean the air fryer and 200 amazingly easy recipes for fast & healthy meals that anyone can cook.

Enjoy it!

Chapter 1

Air Fryer Basics

Since air fryers appeared, there has been much speculation about their use and guarantees, so the first thing I will clarify for you is what an air fryer is.

If the term Air Fryer sounds like much hot air, your speculations are exactly correct! A better Taurus air fryer is simply a revolutionized kitchen appliance for cooking food through the circulation of superheated air. It is a new Philips invention that offers healthy and tasty food with less oil.

Deep fryers use Rapid Air technology to cook any food that would otherwise soak it in fat. This new technology works by circulating air at high degrees to fry foods such as fish, potatoes, cakes, chicken, etc.

It is necessary to mention that air fryers are very easy to use, so if you have not had a fryer before, you will learn to use it without significant problems. Usually, you only have to follow a few simple steps to get the fryer up and running and cook your favorite dishes in a much healthier way than with a traditional deep fryer.

How to Use it?

The first thing you may be wondering is how is it possible to fry without oil. And it is a half-truth because although oil is necessary to fry, the amount used for cooking is small.

Therefore, it must be clarified that the name "without oil" that it receives is not entirely real, since it is necessary a little. And its operation for cooking food consists mainly of the circulation of hot air at high speed.

Their use could not be more straightforward. It could be said that they are like a miniature oven and much healthier than cooking with much oil.

An air fryer combines several different cooking methods in one conventional appliance.

- An electrical coil suspended above food provides radiant heating, just like a heater. This dry heat penetrates the food and heats it internally.
- Meanwhile, a fan placed above the coil creates a stream of superheated air that flows around and under the food. This is convection heating, a cooking method often found in commercial ovens.
- The action of frying turns the small amount of oil that is used into a fine mist that coats the food while it circulates. This action mimics the effect of a traditional deep fryer.
- As the hot air flows in, the food's moisture creates the steam needed to finish the cooking process.

Advantages of Air Fryers

- ☐ There is no mess.
- ☐ It is possible to reduce 85% of fat in food.
- ☐ You will cook without fumes or odors in the kitchen or on clothes.
- ☐ You will save on oil since this type of fryers work without oil, although, as I mentioned before, you can add a teaspoon.
- ☐ They do not cause splashing when used.
- ☐ They are easier to clean.

Cooking tips

1. To get golden fries quickly and saving several calories, it is convenient to cook them in two stages at different temperatures, first at 660°F and then at 750°F.
2. 2In the case of chicken wings, crispiness results when the skin is covered with baking powder before frying. (As an additional tip, you should know that the baking powder expands with the heat and forms bubbles around the chicken, achieving the crunchy effect.)
3. For the healthiest, veggies are a hit in the air fryer, especially squash, eggplant, and brussels sprouts that finish tender on the inside and crisp on the outside.

Chapter 2

Breakfast, Snack and Appetizers Recipes

Hemp Seed Porridge

Servings: 3

Preparation time: 10 minutes

Cook time: 15 minutes

Ingredients	Steps to Cook
<ul><li>2 tbsp of flax seeds</li><li>4 tbsp of hemp seeds</li><li>1 tbsp butter</li><li>¼ tsp salt</li><li>1 tsp of Stevia</li><li>½ ground ginger</li></ul>	1. Place the flax seeds and hemp seeds in a bowl that fits in the basket of the air fryer. Sprinkle the seeds with the salt and ground ginger. Next, combine the almond milk and Stevia. Stir the liquid and pour it into the seed mixture. 2. After this, add the butter 3. Preheat the air fryer to 370°F and cook the porridge hemp seeds for 15 minutes. Stir carefully after 10 minutes of cooking. When the time is up, remove the porridge from the hem of the fryer basket pan and chill for 3 minutes.

Nutritional Information:

- Calories: 106
- Carbohydrates: 4.2g

- Fat: 18.2g
- Protein: 5.1g

Scrambled Eggs With Streaky Bacon

Ingredients

- 6 oz. Bacon
- 4 eggs
- 5 tbsp heavy cream
- 1 tsp of butter
- 1 tsp of paprika
- ½ tsp of nutmeg
- 1 tsp of salt
- 1 tsp ground black pepper

Steps to Cook

1. Chop the bacon into small pieces and sprinkle with salt. Stir the bacon gently and strain it into the air fryer basket. Cook the chopped bacon in the fryer preheated to 360⁰F for 5 minutes.
2. Meanwhile, beat the eggs in the bowl and beat well.
3. Sprinkle the beaten egg mixture with the paprika, nutmeg, and ground black pepper.
4. Gently beat the egg mixture.
5. When the time is up, spoon the butter into the chopped bacon and pour in the egg mixture.
6. Add the heavy cream and cook for 2 minutes.
7. Stir the mixture with the help of the spatula until you get the scrambled eggs and cook the dish for another 3 minutes.

Nutritional Information:

- Calories: 387
- Carbohydrates: 2.3g
- Fat: 32.1g
- Protein: 21g

Hash Breakfast

Servings: 4

Preparation time: 8 minutes

Cook time: 8 minutes

Ingredients

- 1 zucchini
- 7 oz cooked bacon
- 4 oz cheddar cheese
- 2 tbsp of butter
- 1 tsp of salt
- 1 tsp ground black pepper
- 1 tsp of paprika
- 1 tsp of ground thyme

Steps to Cook

1. Chop the zucchini into small cubes and sprinkle with the salt, ground black pepper, paprika, coriander, and ground thyme.
2. Preheat the air fryer to 400⁰F and the butter in the air fryer basket tray.
3. Melt it and add the zucchini cubes
4. Cook the zucchini for 5 minutes.
5. Meanwhile, mash the cheddar cheese
6. When the time is up, shake the zucchini cubes carefully and add the cooked bacon
7. Sprinkle the zucchini mixture with the grated cheese and cook for 3 more minutes.

Nutritional Information:

- Calories: 445
- Carbohydrates: 3.5g
- Fat: 36.1g
- Protein: 26.3g

Green Cheddar Soufflé

Servings: 4

Preparation time: 10 min

Cook time: 8 minutes

Ingredients	Steps to Cook
• 5 oz. Cheddar cheese • 3 eggs • 4 tbsp heavy cream • 1 tbsp chives • 1 tbsp of dill • 1 tsp parsley • ½ tsp ground thyme	1. Break the eggs into the bowl and beat them carefully. 2. Add heavy cream and beat for 10 more seconds. 3. Add chives, dill, parsley, and ground thyme. 4. Sprinkle the egg mixture with the grated cheese and stir 5. Transfer the egg mixture into 4 ramekins and place the ramekins in the basket of the air fryer. 6. Preheat the air fryer to 390°F and cook the souffle for 8 minutes.

Nutritional Information:

- Calories: 244
- Carbohydrates: 1.7g

- Fat: 20.6g
- Protein: 13.5g

Bacon Chocolate Chip Cookies

Servings: 6

Preparation time: 15 min

Cook time: 10 minutes

Ingredients	Steps to Cook
<ul><li>1 egg</li><li>4 oz. Cooked bacon</li><li>1 cup of almond flour</li><li>½ tsp of baking soda</li><li>1 tbsp apple cider vinegar</li><li>3 tbsp of butter</li><li>4 tbsp heavy cream</li><li>1 tsp dried oregano</li></ul>	1. Beat the egg in the bowl and beat it 2. Chop the cooked bacon into small cubes and add it to the beaten egg. Then sprinkle the mixture with the baking soda and apple cider vinegar. 3. Add the heavy cream and dried oregano. 4. Add the butter and almond flour and mix well. 5. When the dough is smooth and runny, the dough is cooked. 6. Preheat the air fryer to 400°F. 7. Pour batter into muffin cups. 8. When the air fryer is preheated, place the muffin shapes in the air fryer basket and cook for 10 minutes. When the time is up, and the muffins are made, remove them from the air fryer.

Nutritional Information:

- Calories: 226
- Carbohydrates: 1.8g

- Fat: 20.5g
- Protein: 10g

Egg Omelette

Servings: 6

Preparation time: 10 min

Cook time: 15 minutes

Ingredients	Steps to Cook

Ingredients

- 6 eggs
- 1/3 cup heavy cream
- 1 tomato
- ½ onion
- 1 tbsp of butter
- 1 tsp of salt
- 1 tbsp of dried oregano
- 6 oz Parmesan
- 1 tsp of chili

Steps to Cook

1. Beat the eggs in the basket tray of the air fryer.
2. Chop the tomato and cut the onion
3. Add the vegetables to the egg mixture
4. Pour the heavy cream
5. Sprinkle the liquid mixture with butter, salt, dried oregano, and chili.
6. Then crumble the Parmesan cheese and add it to the mixture as well.
7. Sprinkle the mixture with the silicone spatula.
8. Preheat the air fryer to 375^{0}F and cook the frittata for 15 minutes.

Nutritional Information:

- Calories: 202
- Carbohydrates: 3.4g

- Fat: 15g
- Protein: 15.1g

Chicken Liver Pâté

Servings: 7

Preparation time: 10 min

Cook time: 10 minutes

Ingredients

- 1 lb. Chicken liver
- 1 tsp of salt
- 4 tbsp of butter
- 1 cup of water
- 1 tsp ground black pepper
- 1 onion
- ½ tsp dried coriander

Steps to Cook

1. Chop the chicken liver roughly and place it on the tray of the air fryer basket. Peel the onion and dice it. Pour the water into the air fryer basket pan and add the chopped onion.
2. Preheat the air fryer to 360⁰F and cook the chicken liver for 10 minutes. When the time is up, strain the chicken liver mixture to discard from the liquid.
3. Transfer chicken liver mixture to a blender.
4. Add the butter, ground black pepper, and dried cilantro. Mix the mixture until you get the texture of the pate.
5. Then transfer the liverwurst into the container and serve immediately or store in the fridge.

Nutritional Information:

- Calories: 173
- Carbohydrates: 2.2g
- Fat: 10.8g
- Protein: 16.1g

Roasted Cherry Tomatoes

Servings: 2-4

Preparation time: 5 min

Cook time: 15 minutes

Ingredients

- ½ lb. cherry tomatoes
- 2 teaspoons of Provencal spices/herbs
- 1 clove garlic, minced
- 2 tbsp of olive oil
- 1 tbsp of Modena balsamic oil
- Salt to taste

Steps to Cook

1. Cut the cherry tomatoes in half.
2. Season them with Provencal spices, minced garlic, salt, olive oil, and balsamic.
3. Place the tomatoes in the deep fryer without oil (using the tray-accessory) and leave them to cook for 15 minutes at 350°F. Enjoy!

Nutritional Information

- Calories: 30
- Carbohydrates: 6.6g
- Fat: 0.5g

- Protein: 1.5g
- Sugar: 4.8g
- Cholesterol:0mg

Bread Of Cassava Fluor

Servings: 7

Preparation time: 10 min

Cook time: 35 minutes

Ingredients	Steps to Cook

Ingredients

- 1 cup of cassava
- 1 cup of brown sugar
- 2 tbsp flour
- 1 tsp ground cinnamon
- 1 egg
- ¼ cup oil
- 1 tbsp butter
- ½ tbsp baking powder
- 2 tbsp of refined sugar
- ½ cup milk
- ½ cup of cottage cheese
- guava strips to taste

Steps to Cook

1. Separate the yolk from the white.
2. Beat the egg white, sweetened with refined sugar, and reserve. Line the bottom of the pan with curd and layer with guava strips.
3. Beat the remaining ingredients in a blender or mixer (except yeast).
4. Add the yeast and mix.
5. Add the egg white and mix it with a spoon.
6. Pour into a greased or nonstick round skillet that will fit in the air fryer.
7. With the air fry already preheated for 5 minutes, put it for 35 minutes at a temperature between 320°F and 350°F. After cooling, turn the plate onto a plate and serve.

Nutritional Information:

- Calories: 75.4
- Carbohydrates: 12.3g

- Fat: 2g
- Protein: 1.9g

Avocado Stuffed With Cheese

Ingredients

- 1 avocado
- 4 cherry tomatoes
- 1.7 oz, feta cheese
- 1 chive
- 1 clove garlic
- fresh thyme to taste
- fresh basil to taste
- Salt to taste
- olive oil to taste
- lemon juice to taste

Steps to Cook

1. Dice the tomatoes and feta cheese.
2. Chop the garlic, chives, and thyme well.
3. Mix all the ingredients well and add a tablespoon of olive oil.
4. Cut the avocado in half and remove the pip.
5. Next, we will season the avocado with lemon juice on top,
6. The avocado holes that the pip has left, we will fill with the mixture of tomato, cheese, and spices that we had made at the beginning
7. (If you want, you can also add diced ham or bacon.)
8. Put the two stuffed avocado halves into the Air Fryer (without preheating) and leave to cook for 10 minutes at 350°F.

Nutritional Information

- Calories: 160
- Carbohydrates: 5.8g
- Fat: 14.7g

- Protein: 2g
- Sugar: 0.7g
- Cholesterol:0mg

Gluten-Free Bread

Servings: 4

Preparation time: 10 min

Cook time: 35 minutes

Ingredients	Steps to Cook

Ingredients

- 1 egg
- ½ tbsp of oil
- 2 tbsp of milk or water
- 1 tbsp oatmeal
- 1 tbsp chickpea or coconut flour
- 1 tbsp of sweet powder
- 1 tsp baking powder
- a pinch of salt
- Oil for greasing

Steps to Cook

1. In a small bowl, break the egg and beat slightly.
2. Add all the other ingredients, leaving the yeast last.
3. Grease a bowl that fits the basket of the air fryer.
4. Pour in the bread dough and smooth out with a spatula.
5. Bring that to the air fryer previously preheated at 360°F for 30 minutes or until the base is golden brown and the batter has risen.
6. Turn the bread over and leave it until the other side is also golden, always keeping the bowl covered.

Nutritional Information:

- Calories: 120
- Carbohydrates: 17g
- Fat: 6g
- Protein: 3g

French Toast With Ham And Egg

Ingredients

- 1 toast
- 1 egg
- Grated cheese)
- Dices of ham
- Margarine
- Salt
- Pepper

Steps to Cook

1. Crush the inside of the toast with a teaspoon (leaving a frame of 1-2 cm).
2. On the edge that you have left, spread margarine and sprinkle grated cheese on top (only on the frame!) Crush the cheese a little so that it does not fall when putting it later in the basket of the fryer without oil.
3. Then put an egg on the toast and season it to taste with a little salt and pepper. Finally, add some diced ham to the egg white.
4. Preheat the fryer to 360°F and then carefully insert the toast into the basket of the Air fryer. Let cook for 8 minutes at 360°F and ... ready!

Nutritional Information:

- Calories: 199
- Carbohydrates: 14
- Fat: 12g

- Protein: 8.8g
- Sugar: 1.8g
- Cholesterol: 195mg

Whole Wheat Bread

Servings: 2

Preparation time: 10 min

Cook time: 35 minutes

Ingredients

- 2 eggs
- 2 tbsp of water
- 1 tbsp oatmeal
- 2 tbsp whole wheat flour
- 1 pinch of salt
- 1 tsp chia
- 1 tsp baking powder
- Oil for greasing

Steps to Cook

1. In a small bowl, break the eggs and beat slightly.
2. Add water, flour, salt, and chia.
3. Add the yeast and mix.
4. Lightly grease a bow that fits the basket of the air fryer.
5. Pour the batter and spread with a spatula.
6. Cover the bowl and cook at 360⁰F for 30 minutes or until the bread rises and turns brown.
7. Turn the bread over and keeping the bowl covered, cook until the other side is also golden.

Nutritional Information:

- Calories: 81
- Carbohydrates: 14g
- Fat: 1.1g
- Protein: 4g

Pizza Balls

Servings: 2

Preparation time: 5 min

Cook time: 15 minutes

Ingredients

- Pizza dough (purchased or homemade)
- Crushed tomato
- Tuna
- cheese
- 3 tbsp of butter
- 1 tbsp of oregano
- 2 cloves of garlic

Steps to Cook

1. Roll out the pizza dough and cut it into squares. A little crushed tomato, cheese, and tuna are placed on each piece.
2. Once the ingredients are added, close the pizza pieces until they form a ball.
3. Finally, we varnish the balls with a little warm butter (to which we have previously added a little oregano and minced garlic). Then we put the balls in the air fryer (without preheating) at 360°F for 15 minutes ... and voila!

Nutritional Information:

- Calories: 350
- Carbohydrates: 30g
- Fat: 21g

- Protein: 10g
- Sugar: 8g
- Cholesterol: 160mg

Sandwich

Servings: 1

Preparation time: 5 min

Cook time: 20 minutes

Ingredients

- 2 slices of bread
- Tomato to taste
- cheese to taste
- pepper to taste
- a little tomato sauce

Steps to Cook

1. Add the tomato sauce on one side of each slice of bread. Add the tomato, cheese, pepper between the two pieces of bread, and fix it with a toothpick so that the ingredients of the sandwich do not move.
2. We put the sandwich in the air fryer (previously preheated) for 12 minutes at 340°F ... and voila!
3. You will find a sandwich with crispy toast on the outside and creamy on the inside.

Nutritional Information:

- Calories: 155
- Carbohydrates: 28g
- Fat: 1.9g

- Protein: 6.2g
- Sugar: 3.4g
- Cholesterol: 0mg

Vegan Bread

Ingredients

- 1 cup of warm water
- 1 ½ tsp salt
- 1 tbsp of olive oil
- 2 cups of wheat flour
- 1 cup whole wheat flour (or cornmeal)
- 2 tsp dry organic yeast
- 1 tbsp brown sugar
- August grains to decorate

Steps to Cook

1. In a bowl, mix ¼ cup of water, organic yeast, and brown sugar. Let stand for 10 minutes. Reserve.
2. In another bowl, mix the dry ingredients, add the liquids, and the reserved yeast. Mix everything to form a homogeneous dough. Knead the dough well.
3. Cover the dough and rest in a warm place for 1 hour or until doubled in size.
4. Set the Air Fryer for 5 minutes at 360^{0}F to preheat.
5. Divide the dough into two parts. With the fryer turned off, put the bread in the basket. Let it rest there for 10 minutes.
6. Then set the Air fryer to 10 minutes at 360^{0}F to bake until needed. They come out beautiful and golden!

Nutritional Information:

- Calories:118.9
- Carbohydrates: 20.5g
- Fat: 3.5g
- Protein: 3.6g

French Fried Potatoes

Ingredients

- 1 lb. of potatoes
- 2 tsp of olive oil
- Salt & spices

Steps to Cook

1. Set the fryer temperature to 390°F.
2. Set the timer to 20 minutes.
3. Put the potatoes in the fryer. The capacity of the Rapid Air system allows the potatoes to be cooked as they come from the freezer or refrigerator.
4. Do not forget to stir the potatoes from time to time to get even cooking.
5. Add salt to enjoy this delicious and healthy dish

Nutritional Information:

- Calories: 192
- Carbohydrates: 23g
- Fat: 9g

- Protein: 2g
- Sugar: 0.9g
- Cholesterol: 300mg

Sweet Potato Ball

Ingredients	Steps to Cook

Ingredients

- 1 lb of boiled, peeled, and crushed sweet potatoes.
- 1 ¼ cup powdered sweet tea
- ¾ cup sour tea
- ½ cup of water
- ¼ cup of olive oil tea
- 1 tbsp of chia
- ½ tbsp of salt

Steps to Cook

1. Mix all the ingredients and mix until you get a homogeneous mass.
2. Take small portions and make balls, place on a baking sheet, and bake in the Air Fryer at 400°F for about 20 minutes.
3. Serve immediately.

Nutritional Information:

- Calories: 72
- Carbohydrates: 12.48g
- Fat: 1.53g
- Protein: 1.97g

Onion Rings

Servings: 8

Preparation time: 10 min

Cook time: 10-12 minutes

Ingredients

- 1 large red onion
- 2 cups all-purpose flour
- 6 eggs
- 2 ½ cups breadcrumbs

Steps to Cook

For the onion rings:

- Peel and cut the onion into thick slices (approx. 2 centimeters thick), then separate them into rings.
- Place the flour, beaten eggs in another bowl, and breadcrumbs in the last bowl in one float bowls. Well-cooked and the mixture of chickpea flour, vinegar and water have linked the ingredients.

To bread:

- For EVERY dip ring and cape in this order: Egg mix
- Flour mix
- Egg mix (this is the second time in the egg)
- Flour mix (this is the second time in flour)
- Egg mix (this is the third time in the egg).
- Finally, in the bread crumbs (press to cover well
- Place ALL the coated onion rings on a metal baking sheet and put them in the freezer for at least 30 minutes.

NOTE: You can do this up to a week in advance.

Cooking in the Air Fryer:

- Preheat fryer to 375⁰F
- place the breaded onion rings in a single layer in the air fryer basket and cover with a little spray oil
- Fry for about 10-12 minutes.
- Onion rings are ready when tender, golden brown, and crisp.

Nutritional Information:

- Calories: 192
- Carbohydrates: 23g
- Fat: 9g

- Protein: 2g
- Sugar: 0.9g
- Cholesterol: 300mg

Flat Bread

Servings: 2-4

Preparation time: 10 min

Cook time: 30 minutes

Ingredients

- ¼ cup of warm water
- 1 tbsp of olive oil
- ½ tsp salt
- ½ tbsp baking powder
- 1 to 2 cups Flour for knitting

Steps to Cook

1. Mix the water with the oil, the salt, and the yeast and gradually add the flour until it comes off your hands. Work the dough on a floured surface just until smooth. Let stand for 15 minutes covered with a cloth.
2. Cut in equal parts and give it the shape you want. The more refined it is, the crunchier it will be after grilling.
3. Place on a baking sheet and bake in the Air Fryer at 400°F for about 30 minutes

Nutritional Information:

- Calories: 72
- Carbohydrates: 12.48g
- Fat: 1.53g
- Protein: 1.97g

Onion Bread

Ingredients

- 1 cup of white wheat flour
- ½ cup whole wheat flour
- 1 tbsp of vegetable oil
- 1 tsp salt
- 2 tsp baking powder
- ½ cup of warm water
- ¼ cup green onions, chopped
- ¼ tsp black pepper (optional)

Steps to Cook

1. In a bowl, add the flour, salt, and yeast, mixing well. Add the water gradually, alternating with the oil. Add the ingredients well until you get a smooth and uniform dough. If using black pepper, add last. If desired, you can use other spices or dried herbs of your choice. Add the chopped green onions and mix well with the batter. Reserve.
2. Grease a medium bowl and preheat the air fryer at 360°F for 5 minutes.
3. Place the dough in the greased bowl, cover, and bake for about 10 minutes. After this time, turn the dough over and let it bake on the other side.

Nutritional Information:

- Calories: 161
- Carbohydrates: 27g
- Fat: 3g
- Protein: 4g

Golden Tacos

Servings: 1-2

Preparation time: 5 min

Cook time: 5 minutes

Ingredients

- ½ lb. chicken breast
- Tortillas to taste
- Cream to taste
- Lettuce to taste
- Avocado to taste
- Tomatoes to taste
- Grated cheese to taste
- Tabasco to taste
- Salt to taste
- Olive oil to taste

Steps to Cook

1. Salt the chicken breast. Cut the chicken breast and cook in the air fryer (without preheating) at 350°F for 16 minutes.
2. Once the chicken breast is cooked, crush the meat into small pieces with your hands.
3. Fill the tortillas with the chicken meat that you have minced and roll until they are well closed.
4. To brown the tacos nicely, varnish the outside of the tortillas with a little olive oil. Next, introduce the dowels in the air fryer at 390°F for 6 minutes.
5. To finish, decorate the tacos with cream, chopped salad, tomato pieces, avocado, and grated cheese ... and ready to eat!

Nutritional Information

- Calories: 19
- Carbohydrates: 4g
- Fat: 1g
- Protein: 1g
- Sugar: 0.5g
- Cholesterol: 30mg

Tornado Potatoes

Servings: 2-4
Preparation time: 5 minutes
Cook time: 20-25 minutes

Ingredients

- 4 small potatoes
- ½ tsp of salt
- ½ tsp of pepper
- 1 tsp of garlic powder
- 1 tsp of paprika
- 1 tsp grated Parmesan cheese
- Olive oil
- Wooden skewers

Steps to Cook

1. Enter the skewer in each potato until it comes out to the other side.
2. With one hand, place the sharp knife diagonally on one end of the potato until the knife touches wood, while with the other hand, turn the potato in the opposite direction. In this, cut all the potatoes in the form of a good spiral.
3. Once finished, we stretch the potato along the skewer. Then we will give a few strokes of olive oil on the spirals.
4. On a separate plate, mix salt, pepper, paprika, garlic powder, and striped Parmesan cheese.
5. Next, we will sprinkle the potatoes with the spice mixture, using a teaspoon.
6. Cut the ends of the skewer; in case the skewers are longer than the fryer basket and introduce the potato skewers in the fryer.
7. Let cook at 320°F for 20-25 minutes.

Nutritional Information:

- Calories: 180
- Carbohydrates: 22g
- Fat: 7g
- Protein: 8g

Hash Pancake

Servings: 7

Preparation time: 7 min

Cook time: 9 minutes

Ingredients	Steps to Cook

Ingredients

- 1 tsp of baking soda
- 1 tbsp of apple cider vinegar
- 1 tsp salt
- 1 tsp ground ginger
- 1 cup of coconut flour
- 5 tbsp of butter
- 1 egg.
- ¼ cup of heavy cream

Steps to Cook

1. Combine the baking soda, salt, ground ginger, and flour in the bowl.
2. Next, Take the separate bowl and break the egg there. Add the butter and heavy cream.
3. Use the hand mixer and mix the liquid mixture well.
4. Next, combine the dry mix and the liquid mix and stir until smooth.
5. Preheat the air fryer to 400^{0}F.
6. Next, pour the pancake mix into the basket pan of the air fryer—Cook the pancake hash for 4 minutes.
7. After this, stir the pancake hash well and continue to cook for 5 more minutes.

Nutritional Information:

- Calories: 178
- Fat: 13.3g
- carbohydrates: 10.7g
- Protein: 4.4g

Slices Of Meatloaf

Servings: 6

Preparation time: 10 min

Cook time: 20 minutes

Ingredients	Steps to Cook

Ingredients

- 8 oz *ground pork*
- 7 oz. of *ground beef*
- 1 *onion*
- 1 *egg*
- 1 tbsp of *almond flour*
- 1 tsp of *chives*
- 1 tsp *salt*
- 1 tsp *cayenne pepper*
- 1 tbsp of *dried oregano.*
- 1 tsp of *butter*
- 1 tsp of *olive oil*

Steps to Cook

1. Beat the egg in the large bowl. Add the ground beef and ground pork. After this, add the almond flour, chives, salt, cayenne pepper, dried oregano, and butter. Peel the onion and dice it. Place the chopped onion into the ground beef mixture.
2. Use your hands to make the meatloaf mixture homogeneous.
3. Preheat the air fryer to 350°F.
4. Make the meatloaf shape from the ground beef mixture.
5. Sprinkle the fryer basket with the olive oil inside, and over the meatloaf there.
6. Cook the meatloaf for 20 minutes.

Nutritional Information:

- Calories: 176
- Carbohydrates: 3.4g
- fat: 2.2g
- Protein: 22.2g

Apple Chips

Ingredients

- 1 Apple
- 2 tbsp of water
- juice of half a lemon

Steps to Cook

1. You just have to remove the center of the apple to remove the seeds. Cut the apples into thin slices and mix them with two tablespoons of water and the juice of half a lemon. The apple slices are then allowed to dry while the air fryer/air fryer is preheated to 180°F.
2. To get some dried apple rings, we will cook the apples for 60 minutes at 185°F. If we prefer crispy apple chips, we leave them in the Air fryer for another 45 minutes.

Nutritional Information:

- Calories: 16
- Carbohydrates: 4.2g
- Fat: 0g

- Protein: 0.1g
- Sugar: 3.7g
- Cholesterol: 0mg

Bacon Burger

Ingredients

- ½ tomato
- ½ cucumber
- ½ onion
- 8 oz. of ground beef
- 4 oz. of cooked bacon
- 1 egg
- 1 tsp of butter
- 2 oz. Lettuce leaves
- 1 tsp of ground black pepper
- ½ tsp salt
- 1 tsp of olive oil
- ½ tsp of minced garlic

Steps to Cook

1. Beat the egg in the bowl and add the ground beef.
2. Chop the cooked bacon and add it to the ground beef mixture. After this, add the butter, ground black pepper, salt, and minced garlic.
3. Mix carefully and make the burgers.
4. Preheat the honor to 370⁰F.
5. Drizzle the deep fryer basket with the olive oil inside and place the patties there.
6. Cook the patties for 8 minutes on each side.
7. Meanwhile, finely chop the onion, cucumber, and tomato.
8. Place the tomato, cucumber, and onion on the lettuce leaves.

Nutritional Information:

- Calories: 618
- Carbohydrates: 8.6g
- Fat: 37.4g
- Protein: 59.4g

Potatoes Chips

Servings: 4-6

Preparation time: 20 min

Cook time: 7-10 minutes

Ingredients

- 1/3 lb. of potatoes
- 2 tsp of olive oil
- Salt & spices

Steps to Cook

1. It is essential to leave the thin slices of potatoes 20 minutes in water to lose the starch. Then you have to let them dry well, to be able to put them to cook in the Air Fryer, and they are finally creamy and crispy.
2. In the fryer without oil, introduce a few potatoes at 185^0F for 20 minutes, and well separated to cook well. This way, you get some crispy and delicious homemade chips. Finally, add salt and other spices if you wish (spicy, garlic, pepper ... each to your liking!)

Nutritional Information:

- Calories: 53
- Carbohydrates: 8.4g
- Fat: 1.9g

- Protein: 1.1g
- Sugar: 3.7g
- Cholesterol: 0mg

Patty With Tuna

Servings: 4

Preparation time: 10 min

Cook time: 15 minutes

Ingredients	Steps to Cook

Ingredients

- *Sliced Bread (Without Crust)*
- *Canned Tuna*
- *Oregano to taste*
- *Pepper to taste*
- *Tomato sauce to taste*
- *I egg*

Steps to Cook

1. Prepare the filling. In a bowl or container, add two cans of canned tuna. Add two tablespoons of tomato sauce or fried tomato, also add a little ground pepper and oregano. You can also add if you want some raw or fried onion.
2. Beat an egg well and with a kitchen brush or a spoon, paint the 4 ends of the sliced bread.
3. With your hand or a fork, close the slices, from one corner to another corner.
4. Next, put in the air fryer previously preheated. Cook for 25 minutes at 350°F.

Nutritional Information:

- Calories: 130
- Carbohydrates: 5g
- Fat: 4.9g

- Protein: 15.8g
- Sugar: 0.5g
- Cholesterol: 30.2mg

Flaxseed Porridge

Servings: 4

Preparation time: 5 minutes

Cook time: 8 minutes

Ingredients	Steps to Cook
<ul><li>2 tbsp of sesame seeds</li><li>4 tbsp chia seeds</li><li>1 cup of almond milk</li><li>3 tbsp flax flour</li><li>1 tsp of Stevia</li><li>1 tbsp butter</li><li>½ tsp of vanilla extract</li></ul>	1. Preheat the air fryer to 375°F. 2. Place the sesame seeds, chia seeds, almond milk, flax flour, Stevia, and butter on the tray of the air fryer basket. 3. Add the vanilla extract and cook the porridge for 8 minutes. 4. When the time is up, carefully stirring the porridge and let it rest for 5 minutes. 5. Next, transfer the food into the serving bowls or ramekins. 6. Enjoy!

Nutritional Information:

- Calories: 298
- Carbohydrates: 13.3g
- Fat: 26.7g
- Protein: 6.2g

Omelette With Bacon

Servings: 6

Preparation time: 10 min

Cook time: 13 minutes

Ingredients	Steps to Cook

Ingredients

- 6 eggs
- ¼ cup of almond milk
- ½ tsp of turmeric
- ½ tsp of salt
- 1 tbsp of dried dill
- 4 oz. of bacon
- 1 tsp butter

Steps to Cook

1. Beat the egg in the bowl of the mixer and add the almond milk.
2. Mix the mixture with the help of the mixer until smooth.
3. Add the turmeric, salt, and dried dill.
4. Then cut the bacon.
5. Preheat the air fryer to 360⁰F and place the sliced bacon on the tray of the air fryer basket.
6. Cook the bacon for 5 minutes.
7. After this, turn the bacon on another side and pour the egg mixture over it.
8. Cook the tortilla for 8 more minutes.

Nutritional Information:

- Calories: 619
- Carbohydrates: 1.6g
- Fat: 15.3g
- Protein: 12.9g

Roasted Apple With Yogurt Sauce

Ingredients

- Apples (1 piece per person)
- Cinnamon powder
- Sugar to taste
- Aniseed
- Sugary yogurt or Greek yogurt, etc.
- Vanilla essence to taste
- Honey to taste

Steps to Cook

1. Cut the apple in half with a knife. Leave the skin and remove the seed. Add a little cinnamon powder to the surface of the apple pieces sugar. You can add the sugar 5 minutes before it finishes roasting to caramelize on top.
2. Add the aniseed grain to give it a different touch.
3. Put in the bottom and piece of aluminum foil or silver foil since the apple, when roasted, it will release its juice. Take advantage of this juice to prepare the sauce that you will add to it later.
4. Introduce the apples and set the timer to 10 or 12 minutes at 350°F.

Prepare the yogurt sauce:

5. Pour a plain yogurt into a container; a little of the apple juice you have left in the aluminum foil. A little vanilla essence, although this is optional, and a tablespoon of honey.
6. Mix all ingredients well.

Nutritional Information:

- Calories: 102.6
- Carbohydrates: 25.8g
- Fat: 0.5g
- Protein: 1.6g

Scrambled Egg With Butter

Servings: 4

Preparation time: 10 min

Cook time: 17 minutes

Ingredients	Steps to Cook

- 4 eggs
- 4 tbsp of butter
- 1 tsp salt

1. Cover the basket of the air fryer with the foil and place the eggs there.
2. Next, transfer the basket from the air fryer into the air fryer and cook the eggs for 17 minutes at 320°F.
3. When the time is up - remove the cooked eggs from the air fryer basket and place them in the cold water to cool.
4. After this, peel the eggs and chop them finely.
5. Then combine the chopped eggs with the butter and add salt.
6. Blend until you get a spread texture.
7. Serve the egg butter with the bread

Nutritional Information:

- Calories: 164
- Carbohydrates: 21.67g

- Fat: 8.5g
- Protein: 3g

Egg Cups With Bacon

Servings: 4

Preparation time: 10 min

Cook time: 15 minutes

Ingredients

- 4 eggs
- 6 oz. Bacon
- ¼ tsp salt
- ½ tsp of dried dill
- ½ tsp of pepper
- 1 tbsp of butter

Steps to Cook

1. Whisk the eggs in the mixing bowl
2. Then add the salt, dried dill, and pepper. Mix the egg mixture carefully with the help of the hand mixer
3. Then spread 4 ramekins with the butter
4. Cut the bacon and put it in the prepared ramequins in the form of cups
5. Then pour the egg mixture into the middle of each ramekin with bacon
6. Set the air fryer to 360°F
7. Put the ramequins in the fryer and close it.
8. Cook the dish for 15 minutes
9. When the time is up, you will get slightly crispy bacon and tender egg mixture
10. Remove the egg cups in the fryer and serve.

Nutritional Information:

- Calories: 319
- Carbohydrates: 1.2g
- Fat: 25.1g
- Protein: 21.4g

Coconut Empanadas

Servings: 4

Preparation time: 20 minutes

Cook time: 15-20 minutes

Ingredients

For the filling:
- 2 cups of milk
- ½ cup grated sweetened coconut
- 1/3 cup sugar
- 3 tbsp cornstarch
- 1 pinch of salt
- 3 egg yolks
- 1 tsp coconut extract (optional)

For the empanada dough:
- 2 ¼ cups flour
- 1 pinch of salt
- 2/3 cup vegetable shortening
- 4-6 tbsp of ice water
- ½ cup of sugar

Steps to Cook

1. P For the filling: In a medium saucepan, heat the milk with the grated coconut over medium-low heat until it starts to boil. Remove from the heat and let it cool until it is at room temperature.
2. In a blender or food processor, blend the milk and coconut mixture. Add the sugar, cornstarch, a pinch of salt, and the egg yolks. Blend until everything is well incorporated.
3. Pour the mixture into the saucepan and heat over medium heat, continually stirring until the mixture thickens, about 5 to 8 minutes. Remove from heat and add the coconut extract; let it cool.
4. For the empanada dough: In a large bowl, combine the flour with the pinch of salt. Add the vegetable shortening. Add the water, one tablespoon at a time, until the dough forms a ball.
5. Preheat the air fryer to 350°F.
6. Divide the dough into 2 parts. Roll each piece of dough out onto a floured surface until 1/4-inch thick. Cut the dough into 4- to 6-inch circles. Place 2-3 tbsp of coconut filling in the center of each dough circle. Fold the dough in half and seal the edges well.

7. Arrange the empanadas on a lightly greased baking sheet. Bake the empanadas for 15 to 20 minutes or until the empanadas are lightly golden brown.
8. Sprinkle the patties with sugar. Enjoy with a cup of coffee with milk.

Nutritional Information:

- Calories: 270
- Carbohydrates: 13.3g
- Fat: 24.6g
- Protein: 5.7g

Baked Avocado With Egg

Servings: 2

Preparation time: 8 minutes

Cook time: 15 minutes

Ingredients

- 1 avocado
- ¼ tsp turmeric
- ¼ tsp black pepper
- ¼ tsp salt
- 2 eggs
- 1 tsp butter
- ¼ tsp flax seeds

Steps to Cook

1. Take the deep bowl and combine the turmeric, ground black pepper, salt, and flaxseed. Shake gently to make it homogeneous.
2. After this, cut the avocado into 2 pairs.
3. Whisk the eggs in separate bowls
4. Sprinkle the eggs with the spice mixture
5. Gently lay the eggs in the avocado halves.
6. Put the avocados in the air fryer.
7. Put in the preheated air fryer at 355^0F and close it.
8. Cook the dish for 15 minutes.

Nutritional Information:

- Calories: 288
- Carbohydrates: 9.4g
- Fat: 26g

- Protein: 7.6g
- Sugar: 5g
- Cholesterol: 300mg

Hash With Ham

Servings: 3

Preparation time: 10 minutes

Cook time: 10 minutes

Ingredients

- 5 oz. *Parmesan*
- 10 oz. *Ham*
- 1 tsp of butter
- ½ onion
- 1 tsp ground black pepper
- 1 egg
- 1 tsp of pepper

Steps to Cook

1. Shred the Parmesan cheese
2. Cut the ham into the small strips
3. Peel the onion and dice it.
4. Beat the egg in the bowl and beat with the hand
5. Add the ham strips, butter, diced onion, and butter
6. Sprinkle the mixture with the ground black pepper and paprika. Mix
7. Preheat air fryer to 350°F
8. Transfer the ham mixture to 3 ramekins and sprinkle with the grated Parmesan cheese.
9. Place in the air fryer and cook for 10 minutes

Nutritional Information:

- Calories: 372
- Carbohydrates: 8g
- Fat: 23.7g
- Protein: 33.2g

Egg Tortilla With Mushroom

Servings: 9

Preparation time: 10 minutes

Cook time: 12 minutes

Ingredients	Steps to Cook

Ingredients

- 1 tbsp of flax seeds
- 7 eggs
- ½ cup of cream cheese
- 4 oz of mushrooms
- 1 tsp of olive oil
- 1 tsp of ground black pepper
- ½ tsp of paprika
- ¼ tsp of salt

Steps to Cook

1. Cut the mushrooms and sprinkle them with the salt, paprika, and ground black pepper.
2. Preheat the air fryer to 400°F.
3. Spray the inside of the air fryer basket pan with olive oil and place the sliced mushrooms there.
4. Cook the mushrooms for 3 minutes.
5. Stir carefully after 2 minutes of cooking.
6. Meanwhile, beat the eggs in the bowl.
7. Add the cream cheese and flax seeds.
8. Mix the egg mixture carefully until smooth.
9. Next, pour the tortilla mix into the air fryer basket pan over the mushrooms.
10. Gently stir the tortilla and cook for another 7 minutes.

Nutritional Information:

- Calories: 106
- Carbohydrates: 1.5g
- Fat: 8.7g
- Protein: 5.9g

Breakfast Cloud Eggs

Servings: 2

Preparation time: 8 minutes

Cook time: 4 minutes

Ingredients

- 2 eggs
- 1 tsp of butter

Steps to Cook

1. Separate the eggs into the egg whites and the egg yolks
2. Then beat the egg whites with the help of a mixer until you get firm white peaks.
3. Spread basket tray on air fryer with handle
4. Preheat air fryer to 3000F
5. Make the medium clouds of the whitewash peaks in the basket tray of the prepared air fryer.
6. Place the tray in the basket in the air fryer and cook the cloud eggs for 2 minutes.
7. After this, remove the basket in the air fryer, place the egg yolks in the center of each egg cloud and return the basket to the air fryer.
8. Cook the dish for 2 minutes
9. After this, remove the cooked dish from the basket and serve

Nutritional Information:

- Calories: 80
- Carbohydrates: 0.3g
- Fat: 6.3g
- Protein: 5.6g

Breakfast Cloud Eggs

Servings: 4

Preparation time: 15 minutes

Cook time: 10 minutes

Ingredients

- 1 tbsp of dried dill
- 1 egg
- 1 tsp salt
- 10 oz. Cauliflower
- 1 tsp of olive oil
- 1 tsp of parsley
- ½ tsp of ground white pepper)

Steps to Cook

1. Wash the cauliflower carefully and cut it into small pieces. Put in the blender and mix well.
2. Beat the egg in the cauliflower mixture and continue mixing for 1 more minute.
3. Transfer the mixed cauliflower mixture into the bowl. Sprinkle with salt, dried dill, almond flour, parsley, and ground white pepper.
4. Mix carefully with the help of the spoon
5. Preheat air fryer to 355°F
6. Sprinkle the air fryer basket tray with the olive oil
7. Make fritters from the cauliflower mixture and put them in the basket tray of the air fryer.
8. Close the air fryer and cook the fritters elsewhere and cook for 7 more minutes.
9. When the fritters are cooked, serve them hot.

Nutritional Information

- Calories: 54
- Carbohydrates: 4.8g

- Fat: 3.1g
- Protein: 3.3g

Western-Style Omelette

Servings: 4

Preparation time: 10 minutes

Cook time: 10 minutes

Ingredients	Steps to Cook

Ingredients

- 1 green pepper
- ½ onion
- 5 eggs
- 3 tbsp of cream cheese.
- 1 tsp of olive oil
- 1 tsp of dried coriander
- 1 tsp dried oregano
- 1 tsp of butter
- 3 oz parmesan, grated

Steps to Cook

1. Beat the eggs in the bowl and beat well.
2. Sprinkle with the cream cheese, dried cilantro, and dried oregano. Add the grated Parmesan and butter and mix in the egg mixture.
3. Preheat the air fryer to 360°F.
4. Pour the egg mixture into the air fryer basket tray and place it in the air fryer—Cook the tortilla for 10 minutes. Chop the green pepper and chop the onion. Pour the olive oil into the pan and preheat it well. Add the chopped green pepper and roast it for 3 minutes over medium heat. Add the diced onion and cook the onion for 5 more minutes. Stir the vegetables frequently. Remove the cooked tortilla from the basket tray of the air fryer and place it on the plate. Add the roasted vegetables and serve

Nutritional Information:

- Calories: 204
- Carbohydrates: 4.3g
- Fat: 14.9g
- Protein: 14.8g

Bread With Tomato-Mozzarella Toast

Servings: 2-4

Preparation time: 25 minutes

Cook time: 45 minutes

Ingredients

- Baguette/bread
- 7 cherry tomatoes
- 1 mozzarella
- 1 chive
- 1 clove garlic
- Basil to taste
- Olive oil to taste
- Salt to taste

Steps to Cook

1. Dice all the ingredients and mix with a splash of olive oil.
2. Cut a baguette into slices and cover with the rest of the ingredients. Let it cook in the fryer without oil (Air fryer) for 6 minutes at 390°F (without preheating).
3. You can also use bread rolls instead of the loaf of bread.

Nutritional Information:

- Calories: 228
- Carbohydrates: 15g
- Fat: 15g
- Protein: 9g
- Sugar: 2.2g
- Cholesterol: 28mg

Chicken and Cheddar Cheese Sandwich

Servings: 2

Preparation time: 10 minutes

Cook time: 10 minutes

Ingredients	Steps to Cook

Ingredients

- 2 slices of cheddar cheese
- 6 oz of ground chicken
- 1 tsp of tomato puree
- 1 tsp cayenne pepper
- 1 egg
- ½ tsp of salt
- 1 tbsp of dried dill
- ½ tsp of olive oil
- 2 lettuce leaves

Steps to Cook

1. Combine ground chicken with cayenne pepper and salt. Add the dried dill and stir. Then beat the egg into the ground chicken mixture and stir well with the help of the spoon.
2. Make two medium patties from the ground chicken mixture.
3. Preheat the air fryer to 380°F.
4. Drizzle the fryer basket pan with the olive oil and place the ground chicken patties there.
5. Cook the chicken patties for 10 minutes. Turn the
6. patties to the other side after 6 minutes of cooking.
7. When the time is up, transfer the cooked chicken patties onto the lettuce leaves.
8. Sprinkle with tomato puree and top with cheddar slices

Nutritional Information:

- Calories: 324
- Carbohydrates: 2.3g
- Fat: 19.2g
- Protein: 34.8g

Meat And Egg Patties Roll

Servings: 6
Preparation time: 15 minutes
Cook time: 8 minutes

| Ingredients | Steps to Cook |

Ingredients

- ½ cup almond flour
- ¼ cup of water
- 1 tsp salt
- 1 egg
- 7 oz. Ground beef
- 1 tsp paprika
- 1 tsp ground black pepper
- 1 tsp olive oil

Steps to Cook

1. Preheat the water (bring it to a boil)
2. Combine the almond would with the salt and stir.
3. Add the boiling water and beat carefully until the mixture is homogeneous. Knead the dough and smooth
4. Leave the dough. Meanwhile, combine ground beef with paprika and ground black pepper.
5. Mix the mixture and transfer it to the pan.
6. Roast the meat mixture for 5 minutes over medium heat. Stir frequently.
7. After this, beat the egg in the meat mixture and stir.
8. Cook the ground beef mixture for 4 more minutes.
9. Roll up the dough and cut it into the 6 squares.
10. Put the ground beef mixture in each box.
11. Roll the squares to make the dough sticks
12. Sprinkle the dough sticks with the olive oil
13. Place the prepared dough sticks in the basket on the air fryer.
14. Preheat the air fryer to 3500F and put the egg meat rolls there.

Nutritional Information:

- Calories: 150
- Carbohydrates: 2.5g
- Fat: 9.6g
- Protein: 13g

Beef Sandwich

Servings: 2

Preparation time: 11 minutes

Cook time: 16 minutes

Ingredients	Steps to Cook

Ingredients

- 6 oz of ground beef
- ½ pitted avocado
- ½ tomato
- ½ tsp of chili flakes
- 1/3 tsp of salt
- ½ tsp ground black pepper
- 1 tsp of olive oil
- 1 tsp of flax seeds
- 4 lettuce leaves

Steps to Cook

1. Combine the minced meat with the chili flakes and salt. Add the flax seeds and stir the meat mixture with the help of a fork.
2. Preheat the air fryer to 370°F.
3. Pour the olive oil into the basket tray of the air fryer.
4. Make two patties from the beef mixture and place them on the basket tray of the air fryer.
5. Cook the burgers for 8 minutes on each side.
6. Meanwhile, cut the tomato and avocado.
7. Separate the ingredients into 2 slices.
8. Place the avocado and tomato on two lettuce leaves.
9. Next, add the cooked minced beef patties.
10. Serve sandwiches only hot

Nutritional Information:

- Calories: 292
- Carbohydrates: 5.9g
- Fat: 17.9g
- Protein: 27.2g

Quiche Of Spinach And Cheese

Servings: 6

Preparation time: 15 minutes

Cook time: 21 minutes

Ingredients

- ½ cup of almond flour
- 4 tbsp of water, boiled
- 1 tsp salt
- 1 cup of spinach
- ¼ cup of cream cheese
- ½ onion
- 1 tsp of ground black pepper
- 3 eggs
- 6 oz cheddar cheese, grated
- 1 tsp of olive oil

Steps to Cook

1. Combine the water with the almond flour and add salt. Mix the mixture and knead the soft, non-sticky dough. Next, spray the basket pan of the air fryer with the olive oil inside.
2. Set the air fryer to 375⁰F and preheat.
3. Roll up the dough and place it on the tray of the crust-shaped air fryer basket. Place the air fryer basket tray in the deep fryer and cook for 5 minutes.
4. Meanwhile, chop the spinach and combine it with the cream cheese and ground black pepper.
5. Slice the onion and add it to the spinach mixture. Stir gently. Beat the eggs in the bowl and beat them.
6. When the time is up, and the quiche crust is cooked - transfer the spinach filling into it.
7. Sprinkle the filling with the grated cheese and pour in the beaten eggs.
8. Set the air fryer to 350⁰F and cook the quiche for 7 minutes. Reduce the heat to 300⁰F and cook the quiche for 9 more minutes. Let the cooked quiche cool well and cut it into pieces

Nutritional Information:

- Calories: 248
- Carbohydrates: 4.1g
- Fat: 20.2g
- Protein: 12.8g

Roasted Padron Peppers

Servings: 2

Preparation time: 5 minutes

Cook time: 10 minutes

Ingredients

- Padron peppers
- Olive oil
- Fat salt

Steps to Cook

1. Mix the peppers with 1-2 tablespoons of olive oil and put them to "fry" in the air fryer at 390°F (without preheating) for 10 minutes.
2. After 5 minutes, open the fryer and stir the peppers. In the end, you just have to pour coarse salt on the peppers and voila!

Nutritional Information:

- Calories: 31
- Carbohydrates: 6g
- Fat: 0.3g

- Protein: 1g
- Sugar: 4.2g
- Cholesterol: 0mg

Keto Egg Roll

Ingredients	Steps to Cook

Ingredients

- 6 tbsp coconut flour
- ½ tbsp salt
- 1 tsp paprika
- 1 tsp butter
- 4 eggs
- 1 tsp chives
- 1 tbsp olive oil
- 2 tbsp boiled water, hot

Steps to Cook

1. Put the coconut flour in the bowl. Add salt and boiling water. Mix and knead the soft dough
2. After this, let the dough rest. Meanwhile, break the eggs into the bowl. Add the chives and paprika.
3. Whisk with the help of the hand
4. Then put the butter in the pan and preheat well
5. Pour the egg mixture into the melted butter in a pancake. Then cook the egg pancake for 1 minute on each side. Remove the cooked egg pancake and cut it. Roll the prepared dough and cut it into 4 squares. Put the chopped eggs in the dough squares and roll them in the shape of the sticks. Brush the egg rolls with the olive oil.
6. Preheat air fryer to 355°F. Place the egg rolls in the air fryer—Cook for 8 minutes.

Nutritional Information:

- Calories: 148
- Carbohydrates: 8.2g
- Fat: 10g
- Protein: 7.1g

Baked Chicken Sausages

Servings: 6

Preparation time: 15 minutes

Cook time: 12 minutes

Ingredients

- 7 oz. Ground chicken
- 7 oz. Ground pork
- 1 tsp minced garlic
- 1 tsp salt
- ½ tsp nutmeg
- 1 tsp olive oil
- 1 tbsp almond flour
- 1 egg
- 1 tsp chili flakes
- 1 tsp ground coriander

Steps to Cook

1. Combine ground chicken and ground pork in a bowl
2. Whisk the egg into the mixture
3. Then mix with the help of the spoon.
4. After this, sprinkle the meat mixture with the minced garlic, salt, nutmeg, almond flour, chili flakes, and ground coriander.
5. Mix to make the smooth texture of ground beef.
6. Preheat the air fryer to 360⁰F
7. Make the medium sausages to the ground beef mixture
8. Drizzle the basket tray of the air fryer with the olive oil inside.
9. Place the prepared sausages in the basket of the air fryer and place it in the air fryer.
10. Cook the sausages for 6 minutes on each side.

Nutritional Information:

- Calories: 156
- Carbohydrates: 1.3g
- Fat: 7.5g
- Protein: 20.2g

Blackberry Muffins

Servings: 5

Preparation time: 15 minutes

Cook time: 10 minutes

Ingredients

- 1 tsp of apple cider vinegar
- 1 cup of almond flour
- 4 tbsp of butter
- 6 tbsp of almond milk
- 1 tsp of baking soda
- 3 oz blackberry
- ½ tsp of salt
- 3 tsp of Stevia
- 1 tsp of vanilla extract

Steps to Cook

1. Put the almond flour in the mixing bowl
2. Add the baking soda, salt, Stevia, and vanilla extract.
3. Add the butter, almond milk, and apple cider vinegar
4. Break the berries gently and add them to the almond flour mixture.
5. Stir carefully with the help of the fork until the dough is homogeneous.
6. Leave the cupcake mixture in the warm place for 5 minutes.
7. Preheat air fryer to 400°F. Prepare the cupcake shapes. Next, pour the dough into the cupcake shapes. Fill half of each cupcake shape.
8. When the air fryer is preheated, place the cupcake forms with the filling in the basket on the air fryer. Close the air fryer. Cook the muffins for 10 minutes.

Nutritional Information:

- Calories: 165
- Carbohydrates: 4g
- Fat: 16.4g
- Protein: 2g

Soufflé Omelette

Ingredients

- 2 eggs
- 2 tbsp of dried parsley
- 1 tbsp heavy cream
- ¼ tsp ground chili
- ¼ tsp salt

Steps to Cook

1. Preheat the air fryer to 391⁰F
2. Break the eggs into the bowl and add the heavy cream
3. Whisk mixture carefully until the smooth liquid texture is obtained
4. Sprinkle the egg mixture with the dried parsley, ground chili, and salt.
5. Mix with the help of the spoon
6. Lugo take 2 ramekins and pour the souffle in it.
7. Place the ramequins in the fryer basket and cook for 8 minutes.

Nutritional Information:

- Calories: 116
- Carbohydrates: 0.9g
- Fat: 9.9g
- Protein: 5.9g

Buffalo-Style Cauliflower

Servings: 5

Preparation time: 10 minutes

Cook time: 15 minutes

Ingredients

- 8 oz. Cauliflower
- 6 tbsp of almond flour
- 1 tsp chili
- 1 tsp cayenne pepper
- 1 tsp ground black pepper
- 1 tomato
- 1 tsp minced garlic
- ½ tsp salt
- 1 tsp of olive oil

Steps to Cook

1. Wash the cauliflower carefully and separate it into the medium foil
2. Sprinkle the cauliflower flowers with the salt
3. Chop the tomato approximately and transfer it. Mix the mixture.
4. Preheat air fryer to 350^0F
5. Generously sprinkle cauliflower florets in almond flour
6. Place the coated cauliflower florets in the fryer basket and cook for 15 minutes, stirring the cauliflower flowers every 4 minutes.

Nutritional Information:

- Calories: 217
- Carbohydrates: 10.8g
- Fat: 17.9g
- Protein: 8.4g

Cheese Tots

Servings: 5

Preparation time: 12 minutes

Cook time: 3 minutes

Ingredients

- 1 egg
- ½ cup almond flour
- ½ cup coconut flakes
- 1 tsp thyme
- 1 tsp of ground black pepper
- 1 tsp of paprika

Steps to Cook

1. Beat the egg in the bowl and beat it
2. Combine coconut flour with thyme, ground black pepper, and paprika. Stir carefully.
3. Sprinkle mozzarella balls with coconut flakes
4. Transfer the balls to the beaten egg mixture
5. Cover them in the almond flour mixture
6. Put mozzarella balls in the freezer for 5 minutes.
7. Preheat air fryer to 400°F
8. Put the frozen cheese balls in the preheated air fryer and cook for 3 minutes.

Nutritional Information:

- Calories: 166
- Carbohydrates: 2.8g
- Fat: 12.8g
- Protein. 9.5g

Chicken Sausage Balls

Servings: 5

Preparation time: 10 minutes

Cook time: 8 minutes

Ingredients

- 8 oz. Ground chicken
- 1 egg white
- 1 tbsp dried parsley
- ½ tsp salt
- ½ ground black pepper
- 2 tbsp almond flour
- 1 tsp olive oil
- 1 tsp paprika

Steps to Cook

1. Beat the egg white and combine it with the ground chicken
2. Sprinkle chicken mixture with dried parsley and salt
3. Add the ground black pepper and paprika
4. Stir the dough carefully using the spoon
5. Wet your hands and make the small balls of the ground chicken mixture
6. Sprinkle each sausage ball with the almond flour.
7. Preheat air fryer to 380⁰F
8. Drizzle the basket tray of the air fryer with the olive oil inside and place the sausage balls there.
9. Cook for 8 minutes on each side until golden.

Nutritional Information:

- Calories: 180
- Carbohydrates: 2.9g
- Fat: 11.8g
- Protein: 16.3g

Tofu Scramble

Servings: 5

Preparation time: 15 minutes

Cook time: 20 minutes

Ingredients	Steps to Cook

Ingredients

- 10 oz. Tofu cheese
- 2 eggs
- 1 tsp chives
- 1 tbsp apple cider vinegar
- ½ tsp salt
- 1 tsp ground white pepper
- ¼ tsp ground coriander

Steps to Cook

1. Crumble the tofu cheese and sprinkle with the apple cider vinegar, salt, ground white pepper, and ground coriander. Mix and leave for 10 minutes to marinate
2. Preheat air fryer to 370°F
3. Transfer the marinated grated tofu cheese to the basket tray of the air fryer and cook the cheese for 13 minutes.
4. Meanwhile, beat the eggs in the bowl.
5. When the cheese is done cooking, pour the egg mixture into the grated tofu cheese and stir with the help of the spatula well.
6. When the eggs start to firm, place in the air fryer and cook for an additional 7 minutes.

Nutritional Information:

- Calories: 109
- Carbohydrates: 2.9g
- Fat: 6.7g
- Protein: 11.2g

Chapter 3

Meat (Pork, Beef and Lamb) Recipes

Roasted Pork Ribs

Servings: 5

Preparation time: 30 minutes

Cook time: 30 minutes

Ingredients

- 1 tbsp of *apple cider vinegar*
- 1 tsp *cayenne pepper*
- 1 tsp *minced garlic*
- 1 tsp of *mustard*
- 1 tsp *chili flakes*
- 16 oz *pork ribs*
- 1 tsp *sesame oil*
- 1 tsp *salt*
- 1 tbsp of *paprika*

Steps to Cook

1. Chop the pork ribs more or less. Then sprinkle the pork ribs with cayenne pepper, apple cider vinegar, minced garlic, mustard, and chili flakes.
2. Then, add the sesame oil and salt. Add the paprika and mix in the pork ribs. Leave in the fridge for 20 minutes. After this, preheat the air fryer to 360⁰F.
3. Transfer the pork ribs into the basket of the air fryer and cook for 15 minutes.
4. After this, turn the pork ribs to the other side and cook the meat for 15 more minutes.

Nutritional Information:

- Calories: 350
- Carbohydrates: 0.2g

- Fat: 31.4g
- Protein: 15.5g

Roasted Pork Sticks

Servings: 4

Preparation time: 15 minutes

Cook time: 10 minutes

Ingredients

- 1 tsp dried basil
- 1 tsp of nutmeg
- 1 tsp oregano
- 1 tsp apple cider vinegar
- 1 tsp of paprika
- 10 oz. Pork fillet
- ½ tsp of salt
- 1 tbsp olive oil
- 5 oz parmesan, grated

Steps to Cook

1. Cut pork steak into thick strips
2. Combine ground ginger, nutmeg, oregano, paprika, and salt in a shallow bowl, stir.
3. Sprinkle the pork strips with the spice mixture.
4. Sprinkle the meat with the apple cider vinegar
5. Preheat air fryer to 380°F
6. Sprinkle the basket of the air fryer with the olive oil inside and place the pork strips (sticks) there.
7. Cook for 5 minutes. Turn the pork sticks to the other side and cook for 4 more minutes.

Nutritional Information:

- Calories: 315
- Carbohydrates: 2.2g
- Fat: 20.4g
- Protein: 31.3g

Pork Rinds

Servings: 8

Preparation time: 10 minutes

Cook time: 7 minutes

Ingredients

- 1 lb pork rinds
- 1 tsp of olive oil
- ½ tsp of salt
- 1 tsp chili flakes
- ½ tsp of ground black pepper

Steps to Cook

1. Preheat the air fryer to 365°F.
2. Drizzle the basket tray of the air fryer with the olive oil inside.
3. Next, place the pork rinds in the basket tray of the air fryer.
4. Sprinkle the pork rinds with the salt, chili flakes, and ground black pepper.
5. Mix gently.
6. After this, cook the pork rinds for 7 minutes.
7. When the time is up, gently shake the pork rinds.
8. Transfer the plate to the large container and let it cool for 1 to 2 minutes

Nutritional Information:

- Calories: 239
- Carbohydrates: 0.1g
- Fat: 20.8g
- Protein: 36.5g

Beef Stew

Servings: 6

Preparation time: 15 minutes

Cook time: 23 minutes

Ingredients

- 10 oz short ribs of beef
- 1 cup of chicken broth
- 1 clove garlic
- ½ onion
- 1 carrot
- 1 potato
- 4 oz green peas
- ¼ tsp of salt
- 1 tsp turmeric
- 1 green pepper
- 2 tsp butter
- ½ tsp of chili flakes
- 4 oz. kale

Steps to Cook

1. Preheat the air fryer to 360°F. Place the butter in the air fryer basket pan. Add the short ribs of beef.
2. Sprinkle the short ribs with the salt, turmeric, and chili flakes—Cook the short ribs of veal for 15 minutes.
3. Remove the seeds from the green pepper and slice it. Cut the carrot and potato, slice.
4. Slice the kale and slice the onion. When the time is up, pour the chicken broth over the short ribs of beef. Add the chopped green bell pepper and diced onion, the carrot, and the potato. Sprinkle the mixture with the green peas.
5. Peel the garlic clove and add it to the mixture as well. Mix with the wooden spatula.
6. Next, chop up the kale and add it to the stew mixture. Stir the stew mixture one more time and cook it at 360°F for an additional 8 minutes.

Nutritional Information:

- Calories: 144
- Carbohydrates: 7g
- Fat: 5.8g
- Protein: 15.7g

Rib Steak With Cayenne Pepper

Servings: 2

Preparation time: 10 minutes

Cook time: 13 minutes

Ingredients

- 1 lb. rib steak
- 1 tsp salt
- 1 tsp cayenne pepper
- ½ tsp of chili flakes
- 2 tbsp cream
- 1 tsp of olive oil
- 1 tsp lemongrass
- 1 tbsp butter
- 1 tsp garlic powder

Steps to Cook

1. Preheat the air fryer to 360^0F. Take the shallow bowl and combine the cayenne pepper, salt, chili flakes, lemongrass, and garlic powder. Stir the spices gently. Then sprinkle the rib steak with the spice mixture. Melt the butter and combine it with cream and olive oil.
2. Coat the mixture.
3. Pour the rotated mixture into the air fryer basket pan.
4. Cook the steak for 13 minutes. Do not stir the steak during cooking.
5. Serve the steak. You can cut the steak if you like

Nutritional Information:

- Calories: 708
- Carbohydrates: 2.3g
- Fat: 59g
- Protein: 40.4g

Roasted Slices Bacon

Servings: 4
Preparation time: 15 minutes
Cook time: 10 minutes

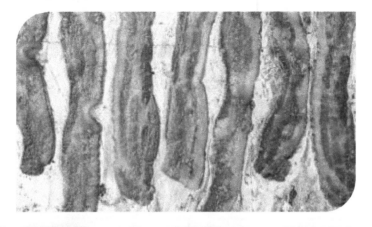

Ingredients

- 8 oz. Bacon
- ½ tsp dried oregano
- ½ tsp salt
- ½ tsp ground black pepper
- ½ tsp ground thyme
- 4 oz. Cheddar cheese

Steps to Cook

1. Cut the bacon and rub it with the dried oregano, salt, ground black pepper, and ground thyme on each side.
2. Leave the bacon for 2 to 3 minutes to soak the spices
3. Preheat air fryer to 3600F
4. Place the sliced bacon on the shelf of the air fryer and cook for 5 minutes.
5. Turn the sliced bacon to the other side and cook for 5 more minutes.
6. Shred the cheddar cheese. When the bacon is cooked, sprinkle with the grated cheese and cook for an additional 30 seconds.

Nutritional Information:

- Calories: 423
- Carbohydrates: 1.5
- Fat: 33.1g
- Protein: 28.1

Roasted Pork Chops

Servings: 3

Preparation time: 10 minutes

Cook time: 11 minutes

Ingredients

- 1 tsp peppercorns
- 1 tsp kosher salt
- 1 tsp minced garlic
- ½ tsp of dried rosemary
- 1 tbsp butter
- 13 oz pork chops

Steps to Cook

1. Rub the pork chops with the dried rosemary, minced garlic, and kosher salt.
2. Next, preheat the air fryer to 365⁰F.
3. Put the butter and peppercorns in the basket tray of the air fryer. Melt the butter.
4. Then place the prepared pork chops in the melted butter.
5. Cook the pork chops for 6 minutes.
6. Then turn the pork chops on another side.
7. Cook the pork chops for 5 more minutes.
8. When the meat is cooked - pat it dry with the help of the paper towel.
9. Serve immediately

Nutritional Information:

- Calories: 431
- Carbohydrates: 0.9g
- Fat: 34.4g
- Protein: 27.8g

Stuffed Beef Heart

Servings: 4

Preparation time: 15 minutes

Cook time: 20 minutes

Ingredients	Steps to Cook

Ingredients

- 1 lb beef heart
- 1 white onion
- ½ cup of fresh spinach
- 1 tsp salt
- 1 tsp ground black pepper
- 3 cups of chicken broth
- 1 tsp of butter

Steps to Cook

1. Prepare the beef heart for cooking: remove all the fat from it. Then peel the onion and dice it.
2. Chop the fresh spinach. Combine the diced onion, fresh spinach, and butter. Stir. After this, cut the heart of the beef and fill it with the spinach and onion mixture.
3. Preheat the air fryer to 400°F.
4. Pour the chicken broth into the air fryer basket tray.
5. Then sprinkle the prepared stuffed veal heart with the salt and ground black pepper. Put the prepared veal heart in the deep fryer and cook for 20 minutes.
6. When time is up - remove the cooked heart from the air fryer and slice. Next, Sprinkle the air fryer slices with the remaining liquid from the air fryer.

Nutritional Information:

- Calories: 216
- Carbohydrates: 3.8g
- Fat: 6.8g
- Protein: 33.3g

Roasted Pulled Pork

Servings: 4

Preparation time: 15 minutes

Cook time: 20 minutes

Ingredients

- 1 tbsp chili flakes
- 1 tsp black pepper
- ½ tsp of paprika
- 1 tsp cayenne pepper
- 1/3 cup of cream
- 1 tsp kosher salt
- 1 lb pork tenderloin
- 1 tsp ground thyme
- 4 cups of chicken broth
- 1 tsp of butter

Steps to Cook

1. Pour the chicken broth into the air fryer basket tray.
2. Add the pork fillet and sprinkle the mixture with the chili flakes, ground black pepper, paprika, cayenne pepper, and kosher salt.
3. Preheat the fryer to 370°F and cook the meat for 20 minutes.
4. After this, strain the liquid and grind the meat with the help of 2 forks. Then add the butter and cream and mix—Cook the pulled pork for 4 more minutes at 360°F.
5. When the pulled pork is cooked, let it cool briefly.

Nutritional Information:

- Calories: 198
- Carbohydrates: 2.3g
- Fat: 6.8g
- Protein: 30.7g

BBQ Beef Jerky

Ingredients

- 14 oz beef flank steak
- 1 tsp of chili
- 3 tbsp apple cider vinegar
- 1 tsp black pepper
- 1 tsp onion powder
- 1 tsp garlic powder
- ¼ tsp of liquid smoke

Steps to Cook

1. Cut the steak into medium pieces and then beat each piece of sliced beef. Take the bowl and combine the apple cider vinegar, ground black pepper, onion powder, garlic powder, and liquid smoke. Beat gently with the help of the fork.
2. Then transfer to the beaten pieces of beef into the prepared mixture and stir well.
3. Leave the meat from 10 minutes to 8 hours to marinate.
4. Next, place the marinated pieces of meat on the shelf of the air fryer.
5. Cook the beef for 2 h 30 minutes at 150⁰F.
6. When beef is cooked - transfer to a serving plate.

Nutritional Information:

- Calories: 129
- Carbohydrates: 1.1g
- Fat: 4.1g
- Protein: 20.2g

Popcorn Pork

Servings: 4

Preparation time: 20 minutes

Cook time: 21 minutes

Ingredients

- 1 lb. pork tenderloin
- 2 eggs
- 1 tsp of butter
- ¼ cup of almond flour
- 1 tsp kosher salt
- 1 tsp of paprika
- 1 tsp ground coriander
- ½ tsp of lemon zest

Steps to Cook

1. Chop the pork tenderloin into large cubes. Then sprinkle the pork cubes with the kosher salt, bell pepper, ground coriander, and lemon zest. Gently mix the meat. Break the egg into the bowl and beat it. Sprinkle the meat cubes with the egg mixture.
2. Coat each pork cube in the almond flour.
3. Preheat the air fryer to 365⁰F.
4. Put the butter in the basket pan of the air fryer and then put the pork bites there.
5. Cook the pork bites for 14 minutes.
6. Turn the pork bites to another side after 7 minutes of cooking.

Nutritional Information:

- Calories: 142
- Carbohydrates: 0.9g

- Fat: 5.4g
- Protein: 21.9g

Cheddar Stuffed Pork Meatballs

Servings: 6

Preparation time: 15 minutes

Cook time: 8 minutes

Ingredients

- 1 lb ground pork
- 5 oz. cheddar cheese
- 1 tbsp dried oregano
- 1 large egg
- ½ tsp of salt
- 1 tsp of paprika
- 1 tbs butter
- ½ tsp of nutmeg
- 1 tsp minced garlic
- ½ tsp of ground ginger

Steps to Cook

1. Break the egg into the bowl and beat it. Then sprinkle the beaten egg with the salt, paprika, nutmeg, and ground ginger. Stir gently and add the ground pork. After this, add the dried oregano and minced garlic. Mix the mixture with the spoon.
2. When you get the meat of homogeneous strength - make 6 medium balls.
3. Cut the cheddar cheese into 6 medium cubes.
4. Fill the pork meatballs with the cheese cubes.
5. Preheat the air fryer to 365⁰F.
6. Place the butter in the air fryer basket pan and melt.
7. Then put the pork meatballs and cook for 8 minutes.
8. Stir the meatballs once after 4 minutes of cooking.

Nutritional Information:

- Calories: 295
- Carbohydrates: 3g
- Fat: 20.6g
- Protein: 23g

Crispy English Bacon

Servings: 4

Preparation time: 7 minutes

Cook time: 10 minutes

Ingredients	Steps to Cook

Ingredients

- ½ tsp of *ground thyme*
- ½ tsp of *ground coriander*
- ¼ tsp of *ground black pepper*
- ½ tsp of *salt*
- 1 tsp of *cream*
- 10 oz *Canadian bacon*

Steps to Cook

1. Slice the English bacon.
2. Combine the ground thyme, ground coriander, ground black pepper, and salt in the shallow bowl, shake gently. Sprinkle the sliced bacon with the spices from each point side.
3. Preheat the air fryer to 360°F.
4. Put the prepared sliced bacon in the deep fryer and cook for 5 minutes. Turn the sliced bacon to the other side and cook for 5 additional minutes.
5. When the bacon is cooked and becomes a little crisp - remove the bacon from the air fryer and sprinkle with the cream gently

Nutritional Information:

- Calories: 150
- Carbohydrates: 1.9g
- Fat: 6.7g
- Protein: 19.6g

Beef Strips With Zucchini Spirals

Servings: 8

Preparation time: 15 minutes

Cook time: 13 minutes

Ingredients

- 1 tsp thyme
- 1 tsp ground black pepper
- 1 tsp salt
- 1 tsp dried dill
- 1 tsp of mustard
- 4 cups of chicken broth
- 2 lbs beef steak
- 1 garlic clove, peeled
- 3 tbsp of butter
- 1 bay leaf

Steps to Cook

1. Cut the beef brisket into strips. Sprinkle the beef strips with the ground black pepper and salt.
2. After this, chop the tomato roughly and transfer it to the blender. Mix well until smooth.
3. Spray the basket pan of the air fryer with the olive oil inside and place the meat strips—Cook for 9 minutes at 365^{0}F. Stir the beef strips carefully after 4 minutes of cooking.
4. Meanwhile, wash the zucchini carefully and make the spirals of the vegetables with the help of the spiralizer. When it is time to cook the meat - add the zucchini spirals over the meat. Sprinkle with the tomato puree, water, and Italian spices.
5. Cook the dish for 4 more minutes at 360^{0}F.
6. When the time is up and in cooked dishes, stir gently with the help of the wooden spatula

---

Nutritional Information:

- Calories: 226
- Carbohydrates: 35.25g
- Fat: 5.3g
- Protein: 12g

Slices Of Veal Parmesan

Servings: 9

Preparation time: 15 minutes

Cook time: 11 minutes

Ingredients

- 12 oz. beef brisket
- 1 tsp kosher salt
- 7 oz. Parmesan, sliced
- 1 white onion
- 1 tsp turmeric
- 1 tsp dried oregano
- 2 tsp butter

Steps to Cook

1. Cut the beef brisket into 4 slices. Sprinkle each piece of meat with the turmeric and dried oregano. Next, spread the air fryer basket pan with the butter.
2. Put the meat slices there. Peel the white onion and cut it. Layer the sliced onion over the beef slices. Next, make the layer of Parmesan cheese.
3. Preheat the air fryer to 365°F.
4. Cook the beef slices for 25 minutes. When the time is up, and the beef slices are cooked - let the dish cool slightly to make the cheese a bit solid

Nutritional Information:

- Calories: 348
- Carbohydrates: 5g
- Fat: 18g
- Protein: 42.1g

Beef With Broccoli

Servings: 4

Preparation time: 10 minutes

Cook time: 13 minutes

Ingredients	Steps to Cook
• 6 oz. broccoli • 10 oz. beef brisket • 1 white onion • 1 tsp of paprika • 1/3 cup of water • 1 tsp canola oil • 1 tsp of butter • 1 tbsp of flax seeds • ½ tsp of chili flakes	1. Cut the veal brisket into the medium. Next, Sprinkle the veal pieces with the paprika and chili flakes. Mix the meat with the help of your hands. 2. Next, preheat the air fryer to 360°F. 3. Spray the air fryer basket pan with the canola oil. 4. Put the pieces of beef in the basket tray of the air fryer and cook the meat for 7 minutes. 5. Stir once during cooking. Meanwhile, separate the broccoli into the florets. When the time is up, add the broccoli florets to the air fryer basket tray. 6. Sprinkle the ingredients with the flax seeds and butter. Add water. Cut the onion and also add it to the tray of the air fryer basket. Stir gently. Then cook the dish at 265°F for 6 more minutes.

Nutritional Information:

- Calories: 295
- Carbohydrates: 3g

- Fat: 20.6g
- Protein: 23g

Tenderloin Pork Bites

Servings: 6

Preparation time: 15 minutes

Cook time: 14 minutes

Ingredients	Steps to Cook

Ingredients

- 1 lb. of pork
- 6 oz. bacon, sliced
- 1 tsp salt
- 1 tsp turmeric
- ½ tsp of red pepper
- 1 tsp of olive oil
- 1 tbsp of apple cider vinegar

Steps to Cook

1. Cut the pork brisket into the medium bites. Then place the pork bites in the large bowl. Sprinkle the meat with the turmeric, salt, red pepper, and apple cider vinegar. Mix the pork bites carefully and leave for 10 minutes to marinate.
2. Then wrap the pork bites in the sliced bacon. Secure the pork bites with the toothpicks.
3. Preheat the air fryer to 370°F.
4. Place the prepared bacon pork bites on the air fryer pan.
5. Cook the pork trotters for 8 minutes.
6. After this, turn the pork bites on another side. Cook the dish for 6 more minutes.

Nutritional Information:

- Calories: 239
- Carbohydrates: 2.8g
- Fat: 13.7g
- Protein: 26.8g

Garlic Lamb Shank

Servings: 5

Preparation time: 15 minutes

Cook time: 25 minutes

Ingredients

- 17 oz lamb shanks
- 2 tbsp garlic peeled
- 1 tsp kosher salt
- 1 tbsp dried parsley
- 1 tsp chives
- 1 white onion
- ½ cup of chicken broth
- 1 tsp of butter
- 1 tsp dried rosemary
- 1 tsp of nutmeg
- ½ tsp of ground black pepper

Steps to Cook

1. Chop the garlic more or less. Make the cuts in the lamb shank and fill the stakes with the minced garlic.
2. Then sprinkle the lamb shank with the kosher salt, dried parsley, dried rosemary, nutmeg, and ground black pepper. Gently stir the spices into the lamb shank. Next, place the butter and the chicken broth in the basket tray of the air fryer.
3. Preheat the air fryer to 380⁰F.
4. Place the diced onion and chives on the air fryer basket tray. Add the lamb shank and cook the meat for 24 minutes. When the lamb shank is cooked - transfer it to the serving plate and sprinkle with the remaining liquid from the cooked meat

Nutritional Information:

- Calories: 205
- Carbohydrates: 3.8g
- Fat: 8.2g
- Protein: 27.2g

Fragrant Pork Tenderloin

Servings: 3

Preparation time: 20 minutes

Cook time: 15 minutes

Ingredients	Steps to Cook

Ingredients

- ½ tsp of saffron
- 1 tsp sage
- ½ tsp of ground cinnamon
- 1 tsp garlic powder
- 1 tsp onion powder
- 1 lb. pork tenderloin
- 3 tbsp of butter
- 1 garlic clove, minced
- 1 tbsp of apple cider vinegar

Steps to Cook

1. Combine the saffron, sage, ground cinnamon, garlic powder, and onion powder in the shallow bowl. Then shake the spices gently to make them homogeneous. After this, coat the pork tenderloin in the spice mixture. Rub the pork tenderloin with the crushed garlic and sprinkle the meat with the apple cider vinegar.
2. Leave the pork tenderloin for 10 minutes to marinate.
3. Meanwhile, preheat the air fryer to 320°F. Place the pork tenderloin on the fryer pan and butter the meat. Cook the pork for 15 minutes. Ready!

Nutritional Information:

- Calories: 328
- Carbohydrates: 2.2g

- Fat: 16.9g
- Protein: 40g

Gravy Pork Chops

Servings: 4

Preparation time: 15 minutes

Cook time: 17 minutes

Ingredients

- 1 lb. pork chops
- 1 tsp kosher salt
- ½ tsp of ground cinnamon
- 1 tsp white pepper
- 1 cup heavy cream
- 6 oz. white mushrooms
- 1 tbsp butter
- ½ tsp of ground ginger
- 1 tsp ground turmeric
- 1 white onion, minced
- 1 garlic clove minced

Steps to Cook

1. Sprinkle the pork chops with the kosher salt, ground cinnamon, ground white pepper, and ground turmeric.
2. Preheat the air fryer to 375 degrees Fahrenheit.
3. Pour the heavy cream into the air fryer basket tray.
4. Then cut the white mushrooms and add them to the heavy cream. After this, add the butter, ground ginger, minced onion, and minced garlic.
5. Cook the sauce for 5 minutes. Then stir in the cream sauce and add the pork chops. Cook the pork chops at 400°F for 12 minutes.
6. When the time is up, gently stir the pork chops and transfer to the serving plates.

Nutritional Information:

- Calories: 518
- Carbohydrates: 6.2g
- Fat: 42.2g
- Protein: 28g

Chili Lamb Chops

Servings: 6

Preparation time: 20 minutes

Cook time: 10 minutes

Ingredients	Steps to Cook

Ingredients

- 21 oz. lamb chops
- 1 tsp of chili
- ½ tsp of chili flakes
- 1 tsp onion powder
- 1 tsp garlic powder
- 1 tsp cayenne pepper
- 1 tbsp canola oil
- 1 tbsp butter
- ½ tsp of lime zest

Steps to Cook

1. Melt the butter and combine it with the canola oil.
2. Whisk in the liquid and add chili, chili flakes, onion powder, garlic powder, cayenne pepper, and lime zest. Beat well.
3. Then sprinkle the lamb chops with the prepared oily marinade.
4. Leave the meat for at least 5 minutes in the fridge.
5. Preheat the air fryer to 400°F.
6. Place the marinated lamb chops in the air fryer and cook for 5 minutes.
7. After this, open the air fryer and turn the lamb chops on another side.
8. Cook the lamb chops for 5 more minutes.

Nutritional Information:

- Calories: 227
- Carbohydrates: 1g
- Fat: 11.6g
- Protein: 28.1g

Lamb Meatballs

Servings: 7

Preparation time: 10 minutes

Cook time: 14 minutes

Ingredients

- 1 clove garlic
- 1 tbsp butter
- 1 white onion
- ¼ tbsp of turmeric
- 1/3 tsp of cayenne pepper
- 1 tsp ground coriander
- ¼ tsp of bay leaf
- 1 tsp salt
- 1 lb. ground lamb
- 1 egg
- 1 tsp ground black pepper

Steps to Cook

1. Peel the garlic clove and mince it. Combine the minced garlic with the ground lamb. Next, Sprinkle the meat mixture with the turmeric, cayenne pepper, ground coriander, bay leaf, salt, and ground black pepper. Beat the egg into the meat for strength. Then grate the onion and add it in the lamb as well.
2. Mix to make the dough smooth.
3. Next, preheat the air fryer to 400°F.
4. Put the butter in the basket tray of the air fryer and melt. Then make the meatballs from the lamb mixture and place in the basket pan of the air fryer.
5. Cook the dish for 14 minutes.
6. Stir the meatballs twice during cooking

Nutritional Information:

- Calories: 134
- Carbohydrates: 1.8g
- Fat: 6.2g
- Protein: 16.9g

Greek Lamb Kleftiko

Servings: 6

Preparation time: 25 minutes

Cook time: 30 minutes

Ingredients	Steps to Cook

Ingredients

- 2 oz garlic clove, peeled
- 1 tbsp dried oregano
- ½ lemon
- ¼ tbsp of ground cinnamon
- 3 tbsp of frozen butter
- 18 oz. leg of lamb
- 1 cup heavy cream
- 1 tsp bay leaves
- 1 tsp dried mint
- 1 tbsp canola oil

Steps to Cook

1. Crush the garlic cloves and combine them with the dried oregano and ground cinnamon. Mix them. Then chop the lemon. Sprinkle the leg of lamb with the crushed garlic mixture Then rub with the chopped lemon. Combine the heavy cream, bay leaf, and dried mint. Beat the mixture well.
2. After this, add the canola oil and beat one more time. Then pour the cream mixture over the leg of lamb and stir carefully. Let the leg of lamb marinated for 10 minutes.
3. Preheat the air fryer to 380⁰F. Chop the butter and sprinkle on the marinated lamb. Next, place the leg of lamb in the basket tray of the air fryer and sprinkle with the remaining cream mixture.
4. Next, sprinkle the meat with the minced butter.
5. Cook the meat for 30 minutes. When the time is up, remove the meat from the air fryer and sprinkle gently with the remaining cream mixture

Nutritional Information:

- Calories: 318
- Carbohydrates: 4.9g
- Fat: 21.9g
- Protein: 25.1g

Swedish Meatballs

Servings: 6

Preparation time: 15 minutes

Cook time: 11 minutes

Ingredients

- 1 tbsp of almond flour
- 1 lb. ground beef
- 1 tsp parsley
- 1 tsp dried dill
- ½ tsp of nutmeg
- 1 oz. onion, minced
- 1 tsp garlic powder
- 1 tsp salt
- ½ cup of heavy cream
- ¼ cup of chicken broth
- 1 tsp mustard
- 1 tsp black pepper
- 1 tbsp butter

Steps to Cook

1. Put the ground beef and almond flour in the bowl.
2. Next, put the dried dill, dried parsley, ground nutmeg, garlic powder, minced onion, salt, ground black pepper, and mustard.
3. Mix to get the meat of quiet strength. After this, make the meatballs from the beef forcemeat.
4. Preheat the air fryer to 380°F.
5. Put the veal meatballs in the basket tray of the air fryer. Add the butter and cook the dish for 5 minutes. After this, turn the meatballs on another side. Sprinkle meatballs with heavy cream and chicken broth. Cook the meatballs for 6 more minutes. When the meatballs are cooked - serve immediately with the creamy sauce.

Nutritional Information:

- Calories: 227
- Carbohydrates: 2.7g
- Fat: 12.9g
- Protein: 24.6g

Shredded Beef With Herbs

Servings: 6

Preparation time: 15 minutes

Cook time: 23 minutes

Ingredients

- 1 tsp thyme
- 1 tsp ground black pepper
- 1 tsp salt
- 1 tsp dried dill
- 1 tsp of mustard
- 4 cups of chicken broth
- 2 lbs beef steak
- 1 garlic clove, peeled
- 3 tbsp of butter
- 1 bay leaf

Steps to Cook

1. Preheat the air fryer to 360⁰F. Combine thyme, ground black pepper, salt, dried dill, and mustard in the small mixing bowl. Sprinkle the steak with the spice mixture from both sides.
2. Massage the steak with the help of your fingertip to make the meat soak in the spices.
3. Next, pour the chicken broth into the air fryer. Add the prepared fillet of beef and bay leaf—Cook the steak for 20 minutes.
4. When the time is up - strain the chicken broth and discard the steak from the air fryer.
5. Shred the meat with the help of 2 forks and put it back in the basket tray of the air fryer. Add the butter and cook the meat for 2 minutes at 365⁰F.
6. Mix the grated meat carefully.

Nutritional Information:

- Calories: 265
- Carbohydrates: 1.2g
- Fat: 14g
- Protein: 32.4g

Roasted Beef Tongue

Servings: 6

Preparation time: 20 minutes

Cook time: 10 minutes

Ingredients

- 1 lb beef tongue
- 1 tsp salt
- 1 tsp ground black pepper
- 1 tsp of paprika
- 1 tbsp butter
- 4 cups of water

Steps to Cook

1. Preheat the air fryer to 365°F.
2. Place the veal tongue on the air fryer basket tray and add water.
3. Sprinkle the mixture with the salt, ground black pepper, and paprika.
4. Cook the beef tongue for 15 minutes.
5. After this, strain the water from the beef tongue.
6. Cut the beef tongue into strips.
7. Next, place the butter in the air fryer basket pan and add the beef strips.
8. Cook the beef tongue strips for 5 minutes at 360 degrees Fahrenheit.

Nutritional Information:

- Calories: 234
- Carbohydrates: 0.4g
- Fat: 18.8g
- Protein: 14.7g

Bacon With Cabbage

Servings: 4

Preparation time: 10 minutes

Cook time: 15 minutes

Ingredients

- 4 oz. bacon, chopped
- 10 oz. white cabbage, shredded
- ¼ of a white onion, cut into cubes
- ½ tsp of salt
- 1 tsp of paprika
- 1 tsp of butter
- ½ tsp of ground black pepper

Steps to Cook

3. Preheat the air fryer to 360⁰F.
4. Place the chopped bacon on the air fryer basket tray. Sprinkle with salt and paprika-
5. Add the butter and cook the bacon for 8 minutes.
6. After this, add the shredded cabbage, diced onion, butter, and ground black pepper.
7. Stir the mixture carefully and cook for 7 more minutes.
8. When the time is up, and the cabbage is tender, remove and serve.

Nutritional Information:

- Calories: 184
- Carbohydrates: 5.6g
- Fat: 13g
- Protein: 11.6g

Bacon Wrapped Asparagus

Servings: 6

Preparation time: 15 minutes

Cook time: 10 minutes

Ingredients

- 7 oz bacon sliced
- 14 oz asparagus
- 1 tsp salt
- 1 tsp ground black pepper
- 1 tbsp of sesame oil
- 1 tsp of paprika

Steps to Cook

1. Wrap the asparagus in the sliced bacon.
2. Preheat the air fryer to 380^{0}F.
3. Put the wrapped asparagus in the air fryer and sprinkle the vegetables with the salt, ground black pepper, paprika, and sesame oil.
4. Cook the asparagus for 5 minutes.
5. After this, turn the asparagus to the other side and cook for 5 more minutes.
6. Then transfer the cooked dish onto serving plates.
7. Serve the garnish only hot
8.

Nutritional Information:

- Calories: 214
- Carbohydrates: 3.5g
- Fat: 16.2g
- Protein: 13.8g

Corned Meat

Servings: 8

Preparation time: 10 minutes

Cook time: 7 minutes

Ingredients

- 1 onion
- 1 tsp black pepper
- ¼ tsp cayenne pepper
- 1 cup of water
- 1 lb beef
- 1 tsp of butter
- ½ tsp of ground paprika

Steps to Cook

1. Peel the onion and cut it finely.
2. Sprinkle the onion with black pepper, cayenne pepper, and ground paprika.
3. Then add water and mix the onion carefully.
4. Preheat the air fryer to 400⁰F and put the tray with the sliced onion in the air fryer basket.
5. Cook the onion for 4 minutes.
6. After this, remove the pan from the air fryer and add the minced garlic.
7. Mix the onion and meat mixture carefully and return it to the air fryer.
8. Cook the beef mixture for 7 minutes at the same temperature.
9. After this, mix the meat mixture carefully with the help of the fork and cook the ground meat mixture for 8 minutes plus point
10. Then remove the cooked meat from the air fryer and mix gently with the help of the fork. Accompany it with white rice.

Nutritional Information:

- Calories: 310
- Carbohydrates: 4.2g

- Fat: 10.8g
- Protein: 46.4g

Chapter 3

Poultry Recipes

Servings: 6

Preparation time: 15 minutes

Cook time: 18 minutes

Ground Chicken Casserole

Ingredients	Steps to Cook

Ingredients

- 9 oz of ground chicken
- 5 oz bacon, sliced
- ½ onion
- 1 tsp salt
- ½ tsp of black pepper
- 1 tsp of paprika
- 1 tsp of turmeric
- 6 oz cheddar cheese
- 1 egg
- ½ cup of cream
- 1 tbsp of almond flour
- 1 tbsp butter

Steps to Cook

1. Take the tray out of the air fryer basket and spread with the butter. Put the ground chicken in the large bowl and add salt and ground black pepper.
2. Add the paprika and turmeric and stir the mixture well with the help of the spoon.
3. After this, grated cheddar cheese.
4. Beat the egg into the ground chicken mixture until smooth. Then mix the cream and the almond flour.
5. Peel the onion and dice it.
6. Place the ground chicken on the bottom of the air fryer pan. Sprinkle the ground chicken with the diced onion and cream mixture.
7. Then make the layer from the grated cheese and sliced bacon.
8. Preheat the air fryer to 380⁰F.
9. Cook for 18 minutes. When the casserole is cooked - let it cool briefly.

Nutritional Information

- Calories: 396
- Carbohydrates: 3.8g
- Fat: 28.6g
- Protein: 30.4g

Chicken Hash

Ingredients	Steps to Cook

Ingredients

- 6 oz. cauliflower
- 7 oz chicken fillet
- 1 carrot
- 1 potatoe
- 1 tbsp cream
- 3 tbsp of butter
- 1 tsp ground black pepper
- ½ onion
- 1 green pepper
- 1 tbsp of water

Steps to Cook

1. Chop the cauliflower roughly and put it in the blender. Mix carefully until you get the cauliflower rice. Chop the chicken fillet into small pieces.
2. Sprinkle the chicken fillet with the ground black pepper and stir.
3. Preheat the air fryer to 380^0F.
4. Put the prepared chicken in the basket tray of the air fryer, add water and cream and cook for 6 minutes. Reduce the heat of the air fryer to 360^0F.
5. Cut the onion, carrot, potato, and the green pepper. Next, add the cauliflower rice, diced onion, the carrot, potato, and chopped green bell pepper. Add the butter and mix the mixture.
6. Cook the dish for 8 other minutes.

Nutritional Information:

- Calories: 261
- Carbohydrates: 7.1g
- Fat: 16.8g
- Protein: 21g

Fried Chicken Strips

Servings: 4

Preparation time: 10 minutes

Cook time: 12 minutes

Ingredients	Steps to Cook

Ingredients

- 1 tsp of paprika
- ½ tsp of ground black pepper
- 1 tbsp butter
- ½ tsp of salt
- 1 lb chicken fillet
- 1 tbsp cream

Steps to Cook

1. Cut the chicken fillet into strips.
2. Sprinkle the chicken strips with the ground black pepper and salt.
3. Next, preheat the air fryer to 365⁰F.
4. Put the butter on the tray of the air fryer basket and add the chicken strips.
5. Cook the chicken strips for 6 minutes.
6. Then turn the chicken strips to the other side and cook for 5 more minutes.
7. After this, sprinkle the chicken strips with the cream and let it rest for 1 minute.

Nutritional Information:

- Calories: 245
- Carbohydrates: 0.6g
- Fat: 11.5g
- Protein: 33g

Chicken Wrapped In Pandan Leaves

Servings: 4

Preparation time: 20 minutes

Cook time: 10 minutes

ç

Ingredients

- 15 oz chicken
- 1 pandan leaf
- ½ onion cut into cubes
- 1 tsp minced garlic
- 1 tsp chili flakes
- 1 tsp of Stevia
- 1 tsp black pepper
- 1 tsp turmeric
- 1 tbsp butter
- ¼ cup of coconut milk
- 1 tbsp chives

Steps to Cook

1. Cut the chicken into 4 large cubes. Put the chicken cubes in the large bowl. Sprinkle the chicken with the minced garlic, minced onion, chili flakes, Stevia, ground black pepper, chives, and turmeric.
2. Mix the meat with the help of your hands. Then cut the pandan sheet into 4 parts. Wrap the chicken cubes in pandan foil. Pour the coconut milk into the bowl with the wrapped chicken and leave it for 10 minutes.
3. Preheat the air fryer to 380⁰F. Put the pandan chicken in the fryer basket and cook the dish for 10 minutes. When chicken is done - transfer to serving plates and chill for at least 2 to 3 minutes.

Nutritional Information:

- Calories: 250
- Carbohydrates: 3.1g
- Fat: 12.6g
- Protein: 29.9g

Bacon Wrapped Cream Cheese Chicken

Servings: 4

Preparation time: 20 minutes

Cook time: 10 minutes

Ingredients

- 1 lb chicken breast, skinless, boneless
- 4 oz bacon, sliced
- 1 tsp of paprika
- ¼ cup of almond milk
- 1 tsp salt
- ½ tsp of ground black pepper
- 1 tsp turmeric
- 1 tsp fresh lemon juice
- 2 butter spoons
- 1 tsp canola oil

Steps to Cook

4. Lightly beat the chicken breast. Then rub the chicken breast with the paprika, salt, ground black pepper, and turmeric. Sprinkle the chicken breast with fresh lemon juice. Put the butter in the center of the chicken breast and roll-up.
5. Wrap the chicken roll in the sliced bacon and sprinkle the bacon chicken with the almond milk and canola oil.
6. Preheat the air fryer to 380°F.
7. Put the bacon chicken in the basket of the air fryer and cook for 8 minutes. Turn the chicken breast to the other side and cook it for 8 more minutes.
8. Don't worry if the bacon will be too crispy - it gives it the juicy texture of the chicken breast.

Nutritional Information:

- Calories: 383
- Carbohydrates: 2.2g
- Fat: 25.4g
- Protein: 35.1g

Cheesy Chicken Drumsticks

Servings: 4

Preparation time: 18 minutes

Cook time: 13 minutes

Ingredients	Steps to Cook

Ingredients

- 1 lb chicken drumstick
- 6 oz cheese left, sliced
- 1 tsp of dried rosemary
- 1 tsp dried oregano
- ½ tsp of salt
- ½ tsp of chili flakes

Steps to Cook

1. Sprinkle the chicken drumsticks with the dried rosemary, dried oregano, salt, and chili flakes.
2. Gently massage the chicken drumsticks and marinate for 5 minutes.
3. Preheat the air fryer to 370°F.
4. Place the marinated chicken drumsticks on the fryer pan and cook for 10 minutes.
5. Turn the chicken drumsticks on another side and cover with the layer of the sliced cheese.
6. Cook the chicken for 3 more minutes at the same temperature.
7. Next, transfer the chicken drumsticks to the large serving plate.

Nutritional Information:

- Calories: 226
- Carbohydrates: 1g
- Fat: 9.8g
- Protein: 16.4g

Roasted Garlic Chicken

Servings: 4

Preparation time: 20 minutes

Cook time: 16 minutes

Ingredients	Steps to Cook

Ingredients

- 3 oz fresh coriander root
- 1 tsp of olive oil
- 3 tbsp minced garlic
- ¼ tsp of a lemon, sliced
- ½ tsp of salt
- 1 tsp black pepper
- ½ tsp of chili flakes
- 1 tbsp dried parsley
- 1 lb chicken

Steps to Cook

1. Peel the fresh coriander and grate it. Next, combine the olive oil with the minced garlic, salt, ground black pepper, chili flakes, and dried parsley.
2. Coat the mixture and sprinkle the chicken stockings.
3. After this, add the sliced lemon and the grated coriander root.
4. Mix the chicken stockings carefully and let them marinate for 10 minutes in the fridge.
5. Meanwhile, preheat the air fryer to 365⁰F.
6. Place the chicken stockings in the basket tray of the air fryer. Add all the remaining liquid from the chicken stockings and cook the meat for 15 minutes.
7. When the time is up, gently turn the chicken to another side and cook for 1 more minute.

Nutritional Information:

- Calories: 187
- Carbohydrates: 3.6g
- Fat: 11.4g
- Protein: 20g

Servings: 6

Preparation time: 10 minutes

Crispy Fried Chicken Skin

Cook time: 6 minutes

Ingredients	Steps to Cook

Ingredients

- 1 lb chicken skin
- 1 tsp dried dill
- ½ tsp of ground black pepper
- ½ tsp of chili flakes
- ½ tsp of salt
- 1 tsp of butter

Steps to Cook

1. Cut the chicken skin roughly and sprinkle with the dried dill, ground black pepper, chili flakes, and salt.
2. Mix in the chicken skin. Melt the butter and add it to the chicken skin mixture. Mix the chicken skin with the help of the spoon.
3. Next, preheat the air fryer to 360^{0}F.
4. Put the prepared chicken skin in the basket of the air fryer. Cook the chicken skin for 3 minutes on each side, cook the chicken skin more if you want the crispy effect

Nutritional Information:

- Calories: 350
- Carbohydrates: 0.2g
- Fat: 31.4g
- Protein: 15.5g

Air Fryer Crispy Curry Chicken

Servings: 4

Preparation time: 10 minutes

Cook time: 15 minutes

Ingredients	Steps to Cook
<ul><li>1 tsp of olive oil</li><li>1 lb chicken thighs, skinless, boneless</li><li>1 onion</li><li>2 tsp minced garlic</li><li>1 tbsp of apple cider vinegar</li><li>1 tbsp lemongrass</li><li>½ cup of coconut milk</li><li>½ cup of chicken broth</li><li>2 tbsp curry paste</li></ul>	1. Peel the onion and dice it. Next, Combine the chicken and chopped onion in the basket tray of the air fryer. 2. Preheat the air fryer to 365°F. 3. Put the chicken mixture in the deep fryer and cook for 5 minutes. After this, add the minced garlic, apple cider vinegar, lemongrass, coconut milk, chicken broth, and curry paste. 4. Mix the mixture with the help of the wooden spatula—Cook the chicken curry for 10 more minutes at the same temperature. 5. When the time is up, and the chicken curry is cooked, remove it from the fryer and stir once more.

Nutritional Information:

- Calories: 275
- Carbohydrates: 7.2g

- Fat: 15.7g
- Protein: 25.6g

Chicken Meatball Casserole

Servings: 7

Preparation time: 15 minutes

Cook time: 21 minutes

Ingredients	Steps to Cook

Ingredients

- 1 eggplant
- 10 oz ground chicken
- 8 oz ground beef
- 1 tsp minced garlic
- 1 tsp white pepper
- 1 tomato
- 1 egg
- 1 tbsp of coconut flour
- 8 oz parmesan, grated
- 2 butter spoons
- 1/3 cup of cream

Steps to Cook

1. Combine ground chicken and ground beef in a large bowl. Add the minced garlic and ground white pepper. Then beat the egg in the bowl with the ground beef mixture and stir carefully until the batter is homogeneous. Then add the coconut flour and mix.
2. Make the little ground beef meatballs.
3. Preheat the air fryer to 360°F. Then sprinkle the fryer basket pan with the butter and pour in the cream. Peel the eggplant and chop it.
4. Put the meatballs on the cream and sprinkle them with the chopped eggplant. Then cut the tomato and place it on the eggplant. Make the layer of the grated cheese over the sliced tomato. After this, put the casserole in the fryer and cook it for 21 minutes. When the time is up - let it cool down.

Nutritional Information:

- Calories: 314
- Carbohydrates: 7.5g
- Fat: 16.8g
- Protein: 33.9g

Chicken Goulash

Ingredients

- 1 white onion
- 2 green bell peppers, chopped
- 1 tsp of olive oil
- 14 oz ground chicken
- 2 tomatoes
- ½ cup of chicken broth
- 2 garlic cloves, sliced
- 1 tsp salt
- 1 tsp black pepper
- 1 tsp of mustard

Steps to Cook

1. Peel the onion and chop it more or less. Next, spray the basket pan of the air fryer with the olive oil inside—Preheat the air fryer to 365°F.
2. Place the diced onion in the basket tray of the air fryer. Add the chopped green bell pepper and cook the vegetables for 5 minutes. Then add the ground chicken. Chop the tomatoes into the small cubes and add them to the air fryer mix as well.
3. Cook the mixture for 6 more minutes. After this, add the chicken broth, sliced garlic cloves, salt, ground black pepper, and mustard. Mix the mixture carefully to obtain a homogeneous texture.
4. Cook the goulash for 6 more minutes.
5. When done, cut the cooked dish into the bowls.

Nutritional Information:

- Calories: 275
- Carbohydrates: 7.2g
- Fat: 15.7g
- Protein: 25.6g

Turkey Meatloaf

Servings: 12

Preparation time: 15 minutes

Cook time: 25 minutes

Ingredients	Steps to Cook

Ingredients

- 3 tbsp of butter
- 10 oz ground turkey
- 7 oz of ground chicken
- 1 tsp dried dill
- ½ tsp of coriander
- 2 tbsp of almond flour
- 1 tbsp minced garlic
- 3 oz. of fresh spinach
- 1 tsp salt
- 1 egg
- ½ tbsp of paprika
- 1 tsp of sesame oil

Steps to Cook

1. Put the ground turkey and ground chicken in the large bowl. Sprinkle ground poultry mixture with dried dill, ground coriander, almond flour, minced garlic, salt, and paprika. Then grind the fresh spinach and add it to the ground poultry mixture.
2. After this, beat the egg into the meat mixture and mix until the mixture is smooth. Spray the air fryer basket pan with the olive oil.
3. Preheat the air fryer to 350°F. Gently roll the ground beef mixture to make the layer flat. Then place the butter in the center of the meat layer. Next, make the meatloaf shape from the ground beef mixture. Use your fingertips for this step. Place the prepared meatloaf on the tray of the air fryer basket.
4. Cook the dish for 25 minutes.
5. When the meatloaf is cooked - let it cool well.
6. Next, remove the meatloaf from the air fryer basket tray and cut it into portions.

Nutritional Information:

- Calories: 142
- Carbohydrates: 1.7g
- Fat: 9.8g
- Protein: 13g

Turkey Meatballs

Servings: 9

Preparation time: 15 minutes

Cook time: 11 minutes

Ingredients

- 1 lb ground turkey
- 1 tsp chili flakes
- ¼ cup of chicken broth
- 2 tbsp dried dill
- 1 egg
- 1 tsp salt
- 1 tsp of paprika
- 1 tsp of coconut flour
- 2 tbsp heavy cream
- 1 tsp canola oil

Steps to Cook

1. Beat the egg in the bowl and beat with the help of the fork. Add ground turkey and chili flakes.
2. Sprinkle the mixture with the dried dill, salt, paprika, coconut flour, and mix. Make the meatballs from the ground turkey mixture.
3. Preheat the air fryer to 360°F.
4. Spray the air fryer basket pan with the canola oil.
5. Then put the meatballs there—Cook the meatballs for 6 minutes - for 3 minutes on each side.
6. After this, sprinkle the meatballs with the heavy cream. Cook the meatballs for 5 more minutes.
7. When the turkey meatballs are cooked, let them cool for 2 to 3 minutes.

Nutritional Information:

- Calories: 124
- Carbohydrates: 1.2g
- Fat: 7.9g
- Protein: 14.8g

Roasted Chicken Poppers

Servings: 9

Preparation time: 15 minutes

Cook time: 11 minutes

Ingredients

- ½ cup of coconut flour
- 1 tsp chili flakes
- 1 tsp ground black pepper
- 1 tsp garlic powder
- 11 oz chicken breast, boneless and skinless
- 1 tbsp canola oil

Steps to Cook

1. Cut the chicken breast into medium cubes and put them in the large bowl. Sprinkle the chicken cubes with the chili flakes, ground black pepper, garlic powder, and stir well with the palms of your hands. After this, sprinkle the chicken cubes with the almond flour.

2. Shake the bowl in the chicken cubes gently to coat the meat—Preheat the air fryer to 365°F. Sprinkle the air fryer basket pan with the canola oil. Then use the chicken cubes there—Cook the chicken poppers for 10 minutes. Turn the chicken poppers to another side after 5 minutes of cooking. Let the cooked chicken poppers cool gently and serve!

Nutritional Information:

- Calories: 124
- Carbohydrates: 1.2g
- Fat: 7.9g
- Protein: 14.8g

Roasted Whole Chicken With Herbs

Servings: 9

Preparation time: 15 minutes

Cook time: 75 minutes

Ingredients

- A *whole chicken, 6 lbs.*
- *Herbs for seasoning (basil, bay, cayenne, cumin, curry powder, dry mustard powder, oregano, rosemary, sage, and thyme.)*
- *1 tsp kosher salt*
- *1 tsp black pepper*
- *1 tsp paprika*
- *1 tbsp minced garlic*
- *3 tbsp of butter*
- *1 tsp canola oil*
- *¼ cup of water*
- *½ white onion*

Steps to Cook

1. Rub the entire chicken with the kosher salt and ground black pepper and all the herbs inside and out. Then sprinkle with the ground paprika and minced garlic.
2. Peel the onion and dice it. Place the chopped onion inside the entire chicken. Then add the butter.
3. Rub the chicken with the canola oil outside.
4. Preheat the air fryer to 360°F and pour water into the air fryer basket.
5. Then place the rack and put all the chicken there.
6. Cook the chicken for 75 minutes.
7. When the chicken is cooked - it will have a little crispy skin.
8. Cut the cooked dish into portions.

Nutritional Information:

- Calories: 464
- Carbohydrates: 0.9g
- Fat: 20.1g
- Protein: 65.8g

Stuffed Turkey Rolls

Ingredients

- 1 lb. turkey fillet
- 2 tbsp garlic clove, sliced
- 1 tsp apple cider vinegar
- ½ white onion
- ½ tsp of salt
- 1 tsp of paprika
- 1 tsp dried dill
- 1 tsp chives
- 4 tsp of butter

Steps to Cook

1. Cut the turkey fillet into 4 parts. Next, beat each turkey fillet gently. Sprinkle the turkey fillets with the apple cider vinegar, salt, paprika and dried dill.
2. Chop the onion and combine it with the sliced garlic clove. Add the chives and butter. Mix the mixture until it is homogeneous. Next, place the scrambled garlic mixture in the center of each turkey fillet.
3. Roll up the steaks and secure the rolls tightly with the toothpicks.
4. Preheat the air fryer to 360⁰F. Place the turkey rolls on the air fryer basket tray and cook the dish for 12 minutes. Turn the rolls on another side once per cook.

Nutritional Information:

- Calories: 155
- Carbohydrates: 4.5g
- Fat: 20.1g
- Protein: 24.2g

Breast Chicken Stew

Servings: 6

Preparation time: 15 minutes

Cook time: 12 minutes

Ingredients

- 8 oz chicken breast
- 1 white onion
- ½ cup of spinach
- 2 cups of chicken broth
- 5 oz. white cabbage
- 6 oz. cauliflower
- 1/3 cup of heavy cream
- 1 tsp salt
- 1 green pepper
- 1 tsp of paprika
- 1 tsp cayenne pepper
- 1 tsp of butter
- 1 tsp ground coriander

Steps to Cook

1. Cut the chicken breast into large cubes. Sprinkle the chicken cubes with the salt, paprika, cayenne pepper, and ground coriander.
2. Preheat the air fryer to 365°F.
3. Put the butter in the basket tray of the air fryer and melt. Then add the chicken cubes and cook for 4 minutes. Meanwhile, chop the spinach and chop the onion. Then shred the cabbage and cut the cauliflower into small florets.
4. Then chop the green pepper. When the time is up, add all the prepared ingredients to the air fryer basket tray. Pour in heavy cream and chicken broth.
5. Set the fryer to 360°F and cook the stew for 8 more minutes. Stir gently with the help of the spatula.

Nutritional Information:

- Calories: 102
- Carbohydrates: 6.4g
- Fat: 4.5g
- Protein: 9.8g

Ground Chicken Pizza

Servings: 6

Preparation time: 15 minutes

Cook time: 12 minutes

Ingredients

- 10 oz ground chicken
- 1 tsp minced garlic
- 1 tsp of almond flour
- ½ tsp of salt
- 1 tsp black pepper
- 1 large egg
- 6 oz cheddar cheese, grated
- ½ tsp of dried dill

Steps to Cook

1. Put the ground chicken in the bowl. Sprinkle with minced garlic, almond flour, salt, ground black pepper, and dried dill. Then break the egg into the ground chicken mixture and mix it in with the help of the spoon when you get the smooth and homogeneous texture of the ground chicken.
2. Preheat the air fryer to 380°F.
3. Cover the pizza pan of the air fryer with the parchment. Next, place the ground chicken mixture on the pizza pan of the air fryer and make the shape of the pizza crust—Cook the chicken pizza crust for 8 minutes. Next, remove the chicken pizza and sprinkle with the grated cheese generously—Cook for 4 other minutes at 365°F.

Nutritional Information:

- Calories: 244
- Carbohydrates: 1.9g

- Fat: 16.1g
- Protein: 22.9g

Chicken And Eggplant Cheesy Lasagna

Servings: 8

Preparation time: 21 minutes

Cook time: 17 minutes

Ingredients

- 6 oz cheddar cheese, grated
- 7 oz Parmesan cheese, grated
- 2 eggplant
- 1 lb. ground chicken
- 1 tsp of paprika
- 1 tsp salt
- ½ tsp of cayenne pepper
- ½ cup of heavy cream
- 2 tsp butter
- 1 onion cut into cubes

Steps to Cook

1. Spread the butter on the tray of the air fryer basket. Then peel the eggplant and cut them. Separate the sliced eggplant into 3 parts.
2. Combine ground chicken with paprika, salt, cayenne pepper, and diced onion. Mix the mixture.
3. Separate the ground chicken mixture into 2 parts.
4. Make the layer of the first part of the sliced eggplant on the tray of the air fryer basket. Next, layer the ground chicken mixture.
5. Sprinkle the layer of ground chicken with half of the grated cheddar cheese. Then top the cheese with the second part of the sliced eggplant. The next step is to layer the ground chicken and all the shredded cheddar cheese. Cover the cheese layer with the last piece of the sliced eggplant. Then, sprinkle with grated Parmesan cheese. Pour in the heavy cream and add the butter.
6. Preheat the air fryer to 365⁰F. Cook the lasagna for 17 minutes.

Nutritional Information:

- Calories: 348
- Carbohydrates: 10.9g
- Fat: 20.6g
- Protein: 31.4g

Sweet Sour Chicken Breas

Servings: 4

Preparation time: 20 minutes

Cook time: 12 minutes

Ingredients	Steps to Cook

Ingredients

- 1 lb. chicken breast, boneless, skinless
- 3 tbsp Stevia extract
- 1 tsp white pepper
- ½ tsp of paprika
- 1 tsp cayenne pepper
- 1 tsp lemongrass
- 1 tsp lemon zest
- 1 tbsp of apple cider vinegar
- 1 tbsp butter

Steps to Cook

4. Sprinkle the chicken breast with the apple cider vinegar. After this, rub the chicken breast with the ground white pepper, paprika, cayenne pepper, lemongrass, and lemon zest.
5. Leave the chicken breast for 5 minutes to marinate.
6. After this, rub the chicken breast with the Stevia extract and leave it for 5 more minutes.
7. Preheat air fryers to 380°F.
8. Rub the prepared chicken breast with the butter and place it on the tray of the air fryer basket.
9. Cook the chicken breast for 12 minutes.
10. Turn the chicken breast to another side after 6 minutes of cooking.

Nutritional Information:

- Calories: 160
- Carbohydrates: 1g
- Fat: 5.9g
- Protein: 24.2g

Duck Legs With Lemon

Servings: 6

Preparation time: 25 minutes

Cook time: 25 minutes

Ingredients	Steps to Cook

Ingredients

- 1 lemon
- 2 lb. duck legs
- 1 tsp ground coriander
- 1 tsp ground nutmeg
- 1 tsp kosher salt
- ½ tsp of dried rosemary
- 1 tbsp of olive oil
- 1 tsp of Stevia extract
- ¼ tsp of sage

Steps to Cook

1. Squeeze the lemon juice and grate the zest. Combine lemon juice and lemon zest in a large bowl.
2. Add the ground coriander, ground nutmeg, kosher salt, dried rosemary, and sage. Sprinkle the liquid with the olive oil and the Stevia extract.
3. Beat carefully and put the duck feet there.
4. Stir the duck legs and leave for 15 minutes to marinate.
5. Meanwhile, preheat the air fryer to 380^0F.
6. Put the marinated duck legs in the deep fryer and cook for 25 minutes. Turn the duck feet to another side after 15 minutes of cooking.

Nutritional Information:

- Calories: 296
- Carbohydrates: 1.6g
- Fat: 11.5g
- Protein: 44.2g

Chicken Kebab

Servings: 5

Preparation time: 15 minutes

Cook time: 10 minutes

Ingredients

- 14 oz. chicken fillet
- ½ cup of heavy cream
- 1 tsp kosher salt
- ½ tsp of ground black pepper
- 1 tsp turmeric
- 1 tsp curry powder
- 1 tsp of olive oil

Steps to Cook

1. Combine the heavy cream with the kosher salt, ground black pepper, turmeric, and curry powder.
2. Beat the mixture well.
3. Add the oil and praise it again.
4. Cut the chicken fillet into pieces.
5. Add the chicken pieces to the prepared heavy cream mixture and stir carefully.
6. Preheat the air fryer to 360°F.
7. Put the chicken kebab on the fryer shelf and cook for 10 minutes.

Nutritional Information:

- Calories: 204
- Carbohydrates: 1g
- Fat: 11.4g
- Protein: 23.3g

Chapter 4

Seafood Recipes

Salmon Pie With Egg

Servings: 8

Preparation time: 20 minutes

Cook time: 30 minutes

Ingredients	Steps to Cook
<ul><li>½ cup of cream</li><li>1 ½ cups of almond flour</li><li>½ tsp of baking soda</li><li>1 tbsp of apple cider vinegar</li><li>1 onion cut into cubes</li><li>1 lb salmon</li><li>1 tbsp chives</li><li>1 tsp dried oregano</li><li>1 tsp dried dill</li><li>1 tsp of butter</li><li>1 egg</li><li>1 tsp dried parsley</li><li>1 tbsp ground paprika</li></ul>	<ol><li>Beat the egg in the bowl and beat it.</li><li>Then add the cream and keep beating for 2 more minutes.</li><li>After this, add baking soda and apple cider vinegar.</li><li>Add the almond flour and knead the dough smooth and not sticky.</li><li>Then cut the salmon into small pieces.</li><li>Sprinkle the chopped salmon with the diced onion, chives, dried oregano, dried dill, dried parsley, and ground paprika. Mix well.</li><li>Next, cut the dough into 2 parts.</li><li>Cover the pan of the air fryer basket with the parchment.</li><li>Put the first part of the dough on the tray of the air fryer basket. And make the crust out of it with your fingertips.</li><li>Then add the salmon filling.</li></ol>

11. Roll the second part of the dough with the help of the rolling pin and cover the salmon filling.
12. Set the edges of the cake.
13. Preheat the air fryer to 360°F.
14. Place the air fryer basket tray in the fryer and cook the cake for 15 minutes.
15. After that, reduce the power to 355°F and cook the cake for 15 more minutes.

Nutritional Information:

- Calories: 134
- Carbohydrates: 3.3g

- Fat: 8.1g
- Protein: 13.2g

Salmon Casserole

Servings: 8

Preparation time: 20 minutes

Cook time: 12 minutes

Ingredients

- 7 oz cheddar cheese, grated
- ½ cup of cream
- 1 lb. salmon fillet
- 1 tbsp dried dill
- 1 tsp dried parsley
- 1 tsp salt
- 1 tsp ground coriander
- ½ tsp of black pepper
- 2 green bell peppers, chopped
- 1 onion cut into cubes
- 7 oz bok choy, chopped
- 1 tbsp canola oil

Steps to Cook

1. Sprinkle the salmon fillet with the dried dill, dried parsley, ground coriander, and ground black pepper.
2. Gently massage the salmon fillet and leave it for 5 minutes to let the fish roll the spices.
3. Meanwhile, sprinkle the pan of the air fryer with the canola oil inside. After this, cut the salmon fillet into cubes. Separate the salmon cubes into two parts.
4. Next, place the first part of the salmon cubes on the saucepan tray. Sprinkle the fish with the chopped bok choy, diced onion, and chopped green bell pepper. After this, place the second part of the salmon cubes on the vegetables. Then sprinkle the casserole with the grated cheese and heavy cream.
5. Preheat the air fryer to 380°F.
6. Cook the salmon casserole for 12 minutes.

Nutritional Information:

- Calories: 216
- Carbohydrates: 4.3g
- Fat: 14.4g
- Protein: 18.2g

Asian-Style Roasted Salmon

Servings: 4-6

Preparation time: 10 minutes

Cook time: 20 minutes

Ingredients

- ¼ cup balsamic vinegar
- 1 tbsp rosemary minced
- 2 tbsp Salmon Fillet
- 1 ½ tbsp Sazon Completo
- 1 ½ tbsp ground black pepper
- 2 tbsp olive oil
- ¼ Cup Tamarind Juice Concentrate
- 2 Units garlic mashed
- 1 tbsp sugar
- 1 tbsp rice vinegar
- 1 tbsp soy sauce
- ¼ cup chopped leek
- ½ tbsp sesame oil
- 2 tbsp toasted sesame seeds

Steps to Cook

For the sauce:

1. Mix the tamarind concentrate, garlic, sugar, rice vinegar, soy sauce, leek, *Sazon Completo* MAGGI®, sesame oil, and sesame seeds.
2. Bring the balsamic vinegar and rosemary to the fire, cook until reduced by half. Reserve.
3. Besides, season the salmon with the pepper and half of the olive oil, let it rest for 15 minutes.
4. After a time, heat a grill or pan, grease with the remaining oil, cook for 4 minutes on each side, and garnish with the reserved reduction. Remove from grill and serve with reserved sauce.

Nutritional Information:

- Calories: 323
- Carbohydrates: 10.56g
- Fat: 15.42g
- Protein: 34.1

Servings: 6

Preparation time: 20 minutes

Cook time: 23 minutes

Eggplant And Mushrooms Salad

Ingredients	Steps to Cook

Ingredients

- 1 cup of water
- 1 eggplant
- 6 oz white mushrooms
- 1 clove garlic, sliced
- 2 tbsp apple cider vinegar
- 1 tbsp of olive oil
- 1 tsp canola oil
- ½ tbsp flax seeds
- 1 tsp black pepper
- 1 tsp salt

Steps to Cook

1. Peel the eggplant and cut it into medium cubes.
2. Then sprinkle the eggplant cubes with the half teaspoon of salt.
3. Gently stir the eggplant cubes and leave for 5 minutes.
4. Meanwhile, cut the white mushrooms.
5. Preheat the air fryer to 400°F.
6. Pour water into the basket tray of the air fryer.
7. Add the chopped mushrooms, half a teaspoon of salt, and cook for 8 minutes.
8. Next, strain the water from the mushrooms and cool them.
9. Next, place the eggplant cubes in the air fryer and sprinkle with the canola oil.
10. Cook the eggplants for 15 minutes at 400°F.
11. Stir the eggplants after 7 minutes of cooking.
12. When the aubergines are cooked, let them cool slightly.
13. Combine the aubergines with the chopped mushrooms in the salad bowl.

14. Sprinkle the plate with the flax seeds, olive oil, sliced garlic clove, and ground black pepper.
15. After this, add the apple cider vinegar and stir the salad carefully.
16. Let the salad rest for 5 minutes.

Nutritional Information:

- Calories: 62
- Carbohydrates: 6.9g

- Fat: 3.5g
- Protein: 2g

Tuna In White Wine

Servings: 4

Preparation time: 5 minutes

Cook time: 40 minutes

Ingredients

- 1 lb. tuna in tacos
- 1 leek
- 1 green bell pepper
- 1 clove garlic
- 1 lb. chopped natural tomato
- 2 tbsp of olive oil
- ½ cup of white wine
- 3 bay leaves
- 1 tsp of sugar
- Salt

Steps to Cook

1. Open the jar of chopped natural tomato and drain the liquid.
2. Finely chop the garlic and chop the leek and bell pepper.
3. In a large skillet or casserole, fry the garlic and the leek for 5 minutes and then add the chopped green pepper—salt and cook over low heat for 10 minutes.
4. Then add the bay leaves and the chopped tomato, add the teaspoon of sugar and a little more salt, remove all the sauce, and continue cooking slowly for 15 more minutes. Stir occasionally to prevent sticking.
5. Add the white wine and the previously salted tuna tacos. Cover and leave 10 minutes until the tuna turns white, but without letting it dry.

Nutritional Information:

- Calories: 160
- Carbohydrates: 14.3g
- Fat: 7.6g
- Protein: 9.2g

Crab With White Mushrooms

Servings: 5

Preparation time: 15 minutes

Cook time: 5 minutes

Ingredients

- 7 oz. crab meat
- 10 oz. white mushrooms
- ½ tsp of salt
- ¼ cup of fish broth
- 1 tsp of butter
- ¼ tsp of ground coriander
- 1 tsp dried coriander
- 1 tsp of butter

Steps to Cook

1. Chop the crab meat and sprinkle with the salt and dried coriander. Mix the crab meat carefully.
2. Preheat the air fryer to 400°F.
3. Chop the white mushrooms and combine them with the crab meat.
4. After this, add the fish stock, ground coriander, and butter.
5. Transfer the garnish mixture into the air fryer basket pan.
6. Stir gently with the help of the plastic spatula.
7. Cook the garnish for 5 minutes.

Nutritional Information:

- Calories: 56
- Carbohydrates: 2.6g
- Fat: 1.7g
- Protein: 7g

Mayonnaise Baked Hake

Servings: 3

Preparation time: 10 minutes

Cook time: 20 minutes

Ingredients

- 1 lb. skinless hake fillets (frozen)
- ½ lb. light mayonnaise
- ½ lb. light cream
- 1 tbsp of olive oil
- Pepper to taste
- Salt to taste

Steps to Cook

1. Let the hake fillets thaw at room temperature.
2. Gently clean and pat dry each fillet with a kitchen paper napkin.
3. Add salt and pepper to each fillet on both sides and place them on a baking tray, brush with the tablespoon of olive oil so that the fillets do not stick when cooking.
4. In a bowl, mix the mayonnaise with the liquid cream and a little salt and pepper very well.
5. Next, place the mayonnaise and cream mixture on top of the hake fillets and cook in the oven, previously preheated to 400°F, for 20 minutes.
6. Serve hot accompanied by salad, tomato slices, steamed potatoes, or any other light garnish.

Nutritional Information:

- Calories: 97.7
- Carbohydrates: 2.4g
- Fat: 5.9g
- Protein: 17.4g

Chapter 5

Vegetable Recipes

Roasted Spiced Asparagus

Servings: 6

Preparation time: 9 minutes

Cook time: 6 minutes

Ingredients	Steps to Cook
• 1 lb. asparagus • 1 tsp salt • 1 tsp chili flakes • ½ tsp of ground white pepper • 1 tbsp of sesame oil • 1 tbsp of flax seeds	1. Combine the sesame oil with the salt, chili flakes, and ground white pepper. 2. Coat the mixture. 3. Preheat the air fryer to 400°F. 4. Place the asparagus on the air fryer basket tray and sprinkle with the sesame oil and spice mixture. 5. Cook the asparagus for 6 minutes. 6. When the dish is cooked - let it cool for a few minutes. 7. Serve it

Nutritional Information:

- Calories: 42
- Carbohydrates: 3.4g
- Fat: 2.7g
- Protein: 1.9g

Shirataki Noodles

Servings: 4

Preparation time: 5 minutes

Cook time: 3 minutes

Ingredients

- 2 cups of water
- 1 tsp salt
- 1 tsp Italian seasoning
- 8 oz. shirataki noodles

Steps to Cook

1. Preheat the air fryer to 365^0F.
2. Pour the water into the air fryer basket pan and preheat for 3 minutes. Then add the shirataki noodles, salt, and Italian seasoning.
3. Cook the shirataki noodles for 1 minute at the same temperature. Next, strain the noodles and cook for 2 more minutes at 360^0F.
4. When the shirataki noodles are cooked, let them cool for 1 to 2 minutes. Gently stir the noodles.

Nutritional Information:

- Calories: 16
- Carbohydrates: 1.4g
- Fat: 1g
- Protein: 0g

Roasted Cauliflower Rice

Servings: 6

Preparation time: 8 minutes

Cook time: 10 minutes

Ingredients	Steps to Cook

Ingredients

- 1 white onion cut into cubes
- 3 tbsp of butter
- 1 tsp salt
- 1 lb. cauliflower
- 1 tsp minced garlic
- 1 tsp ground ginger
- 1 cup of chicken broth

Steps to Cook

1. Wash the cauliflower and chop it roughly.
2. Next, put the chopped cauliflower in the blender and blend until you get the rice texture of cauliflower. Transfer the cauliflower rice to the mixing bowl. Add the diced onion.
3. After this, sprinkle the vegetable mixture with the salt, turmeric, minced garlic, and ground ginger.
4. Mix.
5. Preheat the air fryer to 370⁰F. Put the cauliflower rice mixture there. Next, add the butter and chicken broth—Cook the cauliflower rice for 10 minutes.
6. When the time is up - remove the cauliflower rice from the air fryer and strain the excess liquid.
7. Stir gently.

Nutritional Information:

- Calories: 82
- Carbohydrates: 6.5g
- Fat: 6g
- Protein: 2g

Zucchini Gratin

Servings: 6

Preparation time: 15 minutes

Cook time: 13 minutes

Ingredients

- 2 zucchini
- 1 tbsp dried parsley
- 1 tbsp of coconut flour
- 5 oz. parmesan cheese, grated
- 1 tsp of butter
- 1 tsp ground black pepper

Steps to Cook

1. Combine the dried parsley, coconut flour, ground black pepper, and grated cheese in the large bowl.
2. Shake gently to make the dough homogeneous.
3. Then wash the zucchini and slice them.
4. Then cut the zucchini to make squares.
5. Spread the air fryer basket pan with the butter and place the zucchini squares there.
6. Preheat the air fryer to 400°F.
7. Sprinkle the zucchini squares with the dried parsley mixture—Cook the zucchini gratin for 13 minutes.
8. When cooked, the zucchini gratin will have a light brown surface color.

Nutritional Information:

- Calories: 98
- Carbohydrates: 4.2g
- Fat: 6g
- Protein: 8.6g

Winter Squash Spaghetti

Servings: 8

Preparation time: 10 minutes

Cook time: 10 minutes

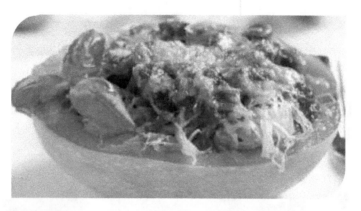

Ingredients	Steps to Cook

Ingredients

- 4 tbsp heavy cream
- 1 cup of chicken broth
- 1 lb. winter squash
- 1 tsp salt
- 1 tsp ground black pepper
- 1 tsp of butter

Steps to Cook

1. Peel the winter squash and grate to get the spaghetti.
2. Preheat the air fryer to 400°F.
3. Put the winter squash spaghetti in the basket tray of the air fryer. Sprinkle in the chicken broth and salt.
4. Add the ground black pepper and cook the dish for 10 minutes. When the time is up - strain the excess liquid from the winter squash spaghetti.
5. Then add the butter and heavy cream and stir.
6. Serve the garnish immediately.
7. Enjoy!

Nutritional Information:

- Calories: 55
- Carbohydrates: 6.4g
- Fat: 3.4g
- Protein: 0.7g

Kale Puree

Servings: 7

Preparation time: 10 minutes

Cook time: 12 minutes

Ingredients	Steps to Cook
<ul><li>1 lb. Italian dark leafy kale</li><li>7 oz. grated Parmesan</li><li>1 tsp salt</li><li>1 cup heavy cream</li><li>1 tsp of butter</li><li>1 tsp ground black pepper</li><li>1 white onion cut into cubes</li></ul>	1. Cut the kale carefully and place it on the air fryer basket tray. 2. Sprinkle the chopped kale with the salt, butter, ground black pepper, diced onion, and heavy cream. 3. Preheat the air fryer to 250°F. 4. Cook the kale for 12 minutes. 5. When the time is up - mix the kale puree carefully to make it homogeneous. 6. Serve the kale puree and enjoy it!

Nutritional Information:

- Calories: 180
- Carbohydrates: 6.8g

- Fat: 13.2g
- Protein: 10.9g

Roasted Celery Stalk

Ingredients	Steps to Cook

Ingredients

- 1 lb. celery size
- 1 tbsp butter
- 1 white onion, sliced
- 1 cup of chicken broth
- 2 tbsp heavy cream
- 1 tsp salt
- 1 tbsp of paprika

Steps to Cook

1. Cut the celery stalk roughly. Pour the chicken broth into the air fryer basket pan and add the sliced onion.
2. Preheat the air fryer to 400°F. Cook the onion for 4 minutes. After this, reduce the heat to 365°F.
3. Add the chopped celery stalk, butter, salt, paprika, and heavy cream. Mix the vegetable mixture.
4. Cook the celery for 8 more minutes.
5. When the time is up - the celery stalk should be very soft.
6. Cool the garnish to room temperature.
7. Serve it and enjoy it!

Nutritional Information:

- Calories: 59
- Carbohydrates: 4.9g
- Fat: 4.2g
- Protein: 1.1g

Servings: 7

Preparation time: 10 minutes

Cook time: 13 minutes

Eggplant Stew

Ingredients	Steps to Cook

Ingredients

- 1 eggplant
- 1 zucchini
- 1 onion
- 1 green pepper
- 2 garlic cloves, peeled
- 1 tsp turmeric
- 1 tsp of paprika
- 1 tsp dried dill
- 1 tsp dried parsley
- 1 cup of vegetable broth
- ½ cup of heavy cream
- 1 tsp kosher salt

Steps to Cook

1. Cut the zucchini and aubergine into cubes.
2. Then sprinkle the vegetables with the dried parsley, dried dill, paprika, and turmeric. Chop the garlic cloves.
3. Then chop the onion and green pepper.
4. Preheat the air fryer to 390°F.
5. Pour the chicken broth into the air fryer and add the eggplants.
6. Cook the eggplants for 2 minutes.
7. After this, add the chopped onion and green pepper.
8. Next, add the minced garlic cloves and heavy cream.
9. Cook the stew for an additional 11 minutes at the same temperature.

Nutritional Information:

- Calories: 65
- Carbohydrates: 8.1g
- Fat: 3.6g
- Protein: 1.7g

Creamy White Mushrooms

Servings: 4

Preparation time: 10 minutes

Cook time: 12 minutes

Ingredients	Steps to Cook

Ingredients

- 9 oz. white mushrooms
- 1 tsp garlic sliced
- 1 onion, sliced
- 1 cup of cream
- 1 tsp of butter
- 1 tsp of olive oil
- 1 tsp ground red pepper
- 1 tsp chili flakes

Steps to Cook

1. Cut the white mushrooms. Sprinkle the white mushrooms with the chili flakes and ground red pepper.
2. Mix the mixture.
3. After this, preheat the air fryer to 400°F.
4. Pour the olive oil into the basket tray of the air fryer.
5. Then add the sliced mushrooms and cook the vegetables for 5 minutes. After this, add the sliced onion, cream, butter, sliced garlic, and mix the mushroom gently with the help of the spatula.
6. Cook the dish for 7 minutes at 365°F.
7. When the time is up, remember the garnish carefully

Nutritional Information:

- Calories: 84
- Carbohydrates: 7g

- Fat: 2.9g
- Protein: 2.9g

Green Bean Puree

Ingredients

- 1 cup green beans
- 6 oz. cheddar cheese, grated
- 7 oz. Parmesan cheese, grated
- ¼ cup of heavy cream
- 1 zucchini
- 1 tsp salt
- 1 tsp of paprika
- ½ tsp of cayenne pepper
- 1 tbsp dried parsley
- 1 tbsp butter

Steps to Cook

1. Cut the zucchini into cubes and sprinkle with the paprika and salt. Next, place the butter in the basket tray of the air fryer. Add the zucchini cubes in the butter.
2. Preheat the air fryers to 400⁰F and cook the zucchini for 6 minutes. Next, add the green beans, grated cheddar cheese, and cayenne pepper.
3. After this, sprinkle the casserole with the grated Parmesan cheese. Pour in the heavy cream.
4. Cook the casserole for 6 more minutes at 400 degrees Fahrenheit. When is cooked - let it cool well

Nutritional Information:

- Calories: 201
- Carbohydrates: 3.3g
- Fat: 15.3g
- Protein: 21.4g

Roasted Cabbage

Servings: 4

Preparation time: 10 minutes

Cook time: 5 minutes

Ingredients	Steps to Cook
<ul><li>9 oz. *white cabbage, sliced*</li><li>1 tsp salt</li><li>1 tsp of butter</li><li>1 tsp of olive oil</li><li>1 tsp of paprika</li><li>½ tsp of ground black pepper</li></ul>	1. Combine the olive oil and the paprika. Melt the butter and add it to the olive oil mixture. After this, add the ground black pepper and fasten it. 2. Rub the sliced white cabbage well with the spice mixture. 3. Then sprinkle the white cabbage slices with the salt. 4. Preheat the air fryer to 400°F. 5. Place the cabbage slices on the fryer rack and cook the dish for 3 minutes. 6. After this, turn the cabbage slices to the other side and cook for 2 more minutes. 7. When the cabbage slices are cooked, they will have a light brown surface.

Nutritional Information:

- Calories: 37
- Carbohydrates: 4.2g
- Fat: 2.3g
- Protein: 0.9g

Creamy Spinach

Servings: 6

Preparation time: 10 minutes

Cook time: 11 minutes

Ingredients	Steps to Cook

Ingredients

- 2 cups of spinach
- 1 cup of cream
- 2 butter spoons
- ¼ cup of coconut milk
- 1 oz. walnuts, crushed
- 5 oz. cheddar cheese shredded
- 1 tsp salt

Steps to Cook

1. Wash the spinach and slice it. Sprinkle the spinach with the salt and mix it to let the spinach give the juice.
2. Next, preheat the air fryer to 380°F.
3. Place the spinach in the basket tray of the air fryer.
4. Add the coconut milk, crushed walnuts, butter, and cream.
5. Cook the spinach for 8 minutes.
6. After this, stir the spinach with the wooden spatula.
7. Add the grated cheese and cook for 3 more minutes.
8. When the time is up, carefully mix the melted cheese and spinach.

Nutritional Information:

- Calories: 209
- Carbohydrates: 2.9g
- Fat: 19.1g
- Protein: 7.9g

Roasted Broccoli With Sriracha

Servings: 5

Preparation time: 10 minutes

Cook time: 6 minutes

Ingredients	Steps to Cook

Ingredients

- 1 tsp sriracha
- 1 tbsp canola oil
- 1 tsp flax seeds
- 1 tsp ground white pepper
- 1 tsp kosher salt
- 1 lb. broccoli
- 4 tbsp vegetable broth

Steps to Cook

1. Wash the broccoli and separate it into the florets.
2. Next, combine the chicken broth, ground white pepper, flax seeds, and sriracha.
3. Add the canola oil and beat the mixture.
4. Preheat the air fryer to 400⁰F.
5. Put the broccoli florets on the fryer basket rack and sprinkle the vegetables with the sriracha mixture.
6. Cook the broccoli for 6 minutes.
7. When the time is up, shake the broccoli gently and transfer it to the serving plates.

Nutritional Information:

- Calories: 61
- Carbohydrates: 6.7g
- Fat: 3.3g
- Protein: 2.7g

Cheesy Cauliflower

Servings: 7

Preparation time: 15 minutes

Cook time: 11 minutes

Ingredients

- 14 oz. cauliflower
- 6 oz. cheddar cheese, sliced
- 1 tsp salt
- 1 tsp ground black pepper
- 1 tsp of frozen butter
- 1 tsp dried dill
- 1 tbsp of olive oil

Steps to Cook

1. Wash the head of cauliflower carefully and cut it into portions. Sprinkle the sliced cauliflower with the salt, ground black pepper, and dried dill.
2. Grate the frozen butter. Next, sprinkle the cauliflower with the olive oil on both sides.
3. Preheat the air fryer to 400°F.
4. Place the cauliflower in the air fryer and cook for 7 minutes. After this, turn the cauliflower on another side and sprinkle with the grated frozen butter. Cook the cauliflower for 3 more minutes.
5. Next, place the cheese on the cauliflower and cook it for another minute.

Nutritional Information:

- Calories: 135
- Carbohydrates: 3.6g
- Fat: 10.7g
- Protein: 7.2g

Roasted Cauliflower

Servings: 6

Preparation time: 10 minutes

Cook time: 15 minutes

Ingredients

- 1 oz. cauliflower head
- 1 tsp onion powder
- ½ cup of heavy cream
- 5 oz. parmesan, grated
- 1 tsp garlic powder
- 1 tsp salt

Steps to Cook

1. Combine heavy cream, onion powder, garlic powder, salt, and grated Parmesan cheese in a large bowl. Mix the mixture. Next, place the cauliflower head in the heavy cream mixture.
2. Cover the cauliflower with the heavy cream mixture with your hands.
3. Next, preheat the air fryer to 360^{0}F.
4. Place the cauliflower head in the fryer basket and cook for 12 minutes.
5. After this, increase the temperature to 390^{0}F and cook the cauliflower head for 3 minutes.

Nutritional Information:

- Calories: 132
- Carbohydrates: 5.8g

- Fat: 8.8g
- Protein: 9.4g

Servings: 8

Preparation time: 10 minutes

Cook time: 12 minutes

Cheesy Zucchini

Ingredients	Steps to Cook

Ingredients

- 3 zucchini
- 1 tbsp canola oil
- ½ tsp of chili powder
- 1 tsp garlic powder
- 6 oz. cheddar cheese shredded

Steps to Cook

1. Cut the zucchini into cubes.
2. Sprinkle the zucchini cubes with eth chili powder, garlic powder, and olive oil.
3. Next, preheat the air fryer to 400⁰F.
4. Place the zucchini cubes in the air fryer and cook the vegetables for 10 minutes.
5. Then sprinkle the zucchini with the grated cheese.
6. Cook the garnish for two more minutes.
7. When zucchini is cooked - transfer it to serving plates.

Nutritional Information:

- Calories: 115
- Carbohydrates: 3.1g
- Fat: 9g
- Protein: 6.3g

Artichoke Stuffed With Spinach

Servings: 5

Preparation time: 15 minutes

Cook time: 40 minutes

Ingredients	Steps to Cook

Ingredients

- 4 tbsp fresh chopped spinach
- ½ tbsp of heavy cream
- 1 tsp of butter
- 1 tsp salt
- 1 lb. artichoke
- 1 tsp of olive oil
- ½ lemon
- 1 tsp ground black pepper

Steps to Cook

1. Prepare the artichokes and remove the core from them. Next, combine the chopped spinach with the heavy cream and butter. Mix the mixture.
2. After this, rub the artichokes with the salt, olive oil, ground black pepper, and half of the lemon.
3. Fill the artichokes with the cream of spinach mixture.
4. Then wrap the artichokes in the foil.
5. Preheat the air fryer to 350⁰F.
6. Put the wrapped artichokes in the basket of the air fryer and cook for 40 minutes.
7. When the time is up, and the artichokes are cooked, discard them from the fryer.
8. Remove foil and serve garnish immediately

Nutritional Information:

- Calories: 66
- Carbohydrates: 10.4g
- Fat: 2.4g
- Protein: 3.2g

Roasted Shredded Brussels Sprouts

Ingredients	Steps to Cook

Ingredients

- 17 oz. brussels sprouts
- 1 oz of butter
- 1 tbsp of olive oil
- 1 tsp ground white pepper
- 1 tsp salt
- 1 tbsp of apple cider vinegar

Steps to Cook

1. Place the brussels sprouts in the blender and crumbled.
   Next, preheat the air fryer to 380°F.
2. Place the grated brussels sprouts on the tray of the air fryer basket. Add the butter, olive oil, ground white pepper, salt, and apple cider vinegar.
3. Mix the grated Brussels sprouts carefully with the help of the spoon.
4. Cook the dish in the preheated air fryer for 15 minutes. When the time is up, remove the plate from the fryer and stir. Serve it immediately.

Nutritional Information:

- Calories: 90
- Carbohydrates: 7.6g
- Fat: 6.4g
- Protein: 2.8g

Cauliflower Rice With Parmesan And Pesto

Servings: 7

Preparation time: 10 minutes

Cook time: 13 minutes

Ingredients	Steps to Cook

Ingredients

- 1 lb. cauliflower head
- 2 tbsp pesto sauce
- 6 oz. grated Parmesan
- 1 tsp salt
- 1 tsp of olive oil
- ½ cup of heavy cream
- 1 tbsp butter
- 1 tbsp dried dill
- 1 tsp dried parsley
- 1 tsp chili flakes

Steps to Cook

1. Wash the cauliflower head carefully and chop it up more or less. Put the chopped cauliflower in the blender and mix well until you get the texture of cauliflower rice.
2. Then place the cauliflower rice in the air fryer and sprinkle with the salt, olive oil, butter, dried dill, dried parsley, and chili flakes. Carefully mix the cauliflower rice with the help of the wooden spatula.
3. After this, add the heavy cream and cook the dish 370^{0}F for 10 minutes.
4. After this, add the grated Parmesan and the pesto sauce. Mix the cauliflower rice carefully and cook it for 3 more minutes at the same temperature.
5. Serve the garnish immediately.

Nutritional Information:

- Calories: 165
- Carbohydrates: 5.1g
- Fat: 12.6g
- Protein: 9.8g

Roasted Bok Choy

Servings: 6

Preparation time: 10 minutes

Cook time: 10 minutes

Ingredients

- 1 white onion, sliced
- 1 lb. bok choy
- 1 tsp minced garlic
- 1 tbsp mustard
- 1 tsp ground ginger
- 2 tbsp apple cider vinegar
- 2 tsp of olive oil
- 1 tbsp butter

Steps to Cook

1. Wash the bok choy cut it. Next, place the chopped bok choy in the basket tray of the air fryer.
2. Sprinkle the minced bok choy with the minced garlic, sliced onion, mustard, ground ginger, apple cider vinegar, olive oil, and butter.
3. Preheat the air fryer to 360°F.
4. Cook the bok choy for 10 minutes.
5. When the dish is cooked - stir carefully.
6. Then let the cooked dish cool slightly.

Nutritional Information:

- Calories: 59
- Carbohydrates: 4.4g
- Fat: 4.2g
- Protein: 1.9g

Servings: 4

Preparation time: 10 minutes

Cook time: 15 minutes

Roasted Green Peppers

Ingredients	Steps to Cook

Ingredients

- 1 tsp minced garlic
- 1 lb. green pepper
- 1 tsp salt
- 1 tbsp of olive oil

Steps to Cook

1. Wash the green peppers carefully and remove the seeds from them. After this, cut the green peppers into the medium squares (or the form you want them).
2. Preheat the air fryer to 320⁰F.
3. Next, place the green pepper squares in the large bowl. Sprinkle the green peppers with olive oil, salt, and minced garlic. Mix.
4. Place the prepared green bell peppers on the air fryer basket tray.
5. Cook the dish for 15 minutes.
6. Stir the green peppers after 8 minutes of cooking.

Nutritional Information:

- Calories: 54
- Carbohydrates: 5.5g
- Fat: 0.6g
- Protein: 1g

Zucchini Boats With Cheese

Servings: 2

Preparation time: 5 minutes

Cook time: 15 minutes

Ingredients

- 1 medium zucchini
- 3 oz bok choy
- 1 clove garlic, sliced
- 6 oz. cheddar cheese
- 4 tbsp heavy cream
- 1 tbsp of coconut flour
- ¼ of salt
- ½ tsp of ground black pepper
- 1 tsp of paprika
- 1 tsp of olive oil

Steps to Cook

1. Cut the zucchini into 2 pieces crosswise. Next, remove the meat from the zucchini halves.
2. Mix the zucchini meat and combine it with the sliced garlic clove. After this, sprinkle the zucchini meat with the salt, ground black pepper, and paprika. Mix. Combine heavy cream and coconut flour and whisk in liquid. Fill the zucchini halves with the zucchini meat mixture. Grind into bok choy and sprinkle with the heavy cream mixture—grated cheddar cheese. Add the bok choy mixture to the zucchini halves. Next, sprinkle the zucchini with the olive oil—Preheat the air fryer to 400ºF.
3. Put the zucchini halves in the deep fryer and cook for 10 minutes. Then sprinkle the zucchini boards with the grated cheese and cook for 2 minutes.

Nutritional Information:

- Calories: 255
- Carbohydrates: 5g
- Fat: 21.2g
- Protein: 12.2g

Parsley Butter Mushrooms

Servings: 5

Preparation time: 10 minutes

Cook time: 7 minutes

Ingredients

- 10 oz. white mushrooms
- 1 white onion, sliced
- 1 tsp of olive oil
- 1/3 of garlic powder
- 3 tbsp of butter
- ½ cup of heavy cream
- 2 tbsp dried parsley
- ½ tsp of salt

Steps to Cook

1. Cut the white mushrooms and sprinkle them with the garlic powder and salt.
2. Preheat the air fryer to 400°F.
3. Place the sliced mushrooms on the air fryer basket tray. Next, sprinkle the mushrooms with the olive oil. Add sliced white onion.
4. Cook the mushrooms for 2 minutes. Then stir the sliced mushrooms carefully. Add the butter and heavy cream. Sprinkle the mushrooms with the dried parsley.
5. Stir the mushrooms carefully and cook for 5 more minutes.

Nutritional Information:

- Calories: 133
- Carbohydrates: 4.5g
- Fat: 12.5g
- Protein: 2.4g

Zucchini Noodles

Servings: 4

Preparation time: 15 minutes

Cook time: 5 minutes

Ingredients	Steps to Cook
• 1 green zucchini • 1 cup of chicken broth • 1 tsp of butter • ½ tsp of salt • ½ tsp of ground white pepper	1. Preheat the air fryer to 400°F. 2. Make the zucchini noodles using the spiralizer. 3. Pour the chicken broth into the air fryer basket tray. 4. Add the chicken broth, salt, and ground white pepper. 5. Cook the zucchini broth for 2 minutes. 6. After this, add the zucchini noodles and cook for 3 minutes. 7. Then strain the chicken broth and add the butter. 8. Mix in the soft zucchini noodles so as not to damage them.

Nutritional Information:

- Calories: 19
- Carbohydrates: 2g

- Fat: 1.2g
- Protein: 0.8g

Cauliflower Puree

Ingredients	Steps to Cook

Ingredients

- 2 butter spoons
- 4 tbsp heavy cream
- 1 lb. cauliflower
- 1 tsp garlic powder
- ½ tsp of salt
- 1 tsp chili pepper
- 1 tsp of olive oil

Steps to Cook

1. Preheat the air fryer to 360⁰F.
2. Chop the cauliflower roughly and place in the basket tray of the air fryer.
3. Sprinkle the vegetables with the garlic powder, salt, chili powder, and olive oil.
4. Cook the cauliflower for 10 minutes.
5. After this, stir the cauliflower gently, add the heavy cream, and cook for 3 more minutes at 390⁰F.
6. Then transfer the cooked soft cauliflower into the blender.
7. Mix well until you get a smooth and smooth texture.
8. Add the butter and stir carefully.

Nutritional Information:

- Calories: 115
- Carbohydrates: 5.6g
- Fat: 10.1g
- Protein: 2.2g

Zucchini Pâté Bites

Servings: 4

Preparation time: 15 minutes

Cook time: 12 minutes

Ingredients

- 2 garlic cloves, minced
- 1 tbsp butter
- 1 tsp salt
- ½ tsp of ground black pepper
- 2 zucchini
- ½ tbsp of olive oil

Steps to Cook

1. Peel the zucchini and grate it.
2. Next, combine the grated zucchini with the salt and ground black pepper.
3. Stir in the zucchini.
4. Preheat the air fryer to 390°F.
5. Place the grated zucchini in the air fryer basket tray, add the olive oil and minced garlic clove and cook for 8 minutes.
6. Then stir the zucchini carefully and add the butter.
7. Cook the zucchini pate for 4 more minutes at 400°F.
8. When the time is up, and the zucchini pâté is smooth and smooth, remove it from the air fryer and cool to room temperature.

Nutritional Information:

- Calories: 59
- Carbohydrates: 4g

- Fat: 4.8g
- Protein: 1.4g

Sweet Sour Chinese Greens

Servings: 5

Preparation time: 10 minutes

Cook time: 10 minutes

Ingredients	Steps to Cook

Ingredients

- 1 tbsp chives
- 1 tsp sesame seeds
- 1 tbsp of apple cider vinegar
- 2 butter spoons
- 1 tbsp canola oil
- ½ tsp of salt
- 8 oz bok choy
- 1 tbsp garlic, sliced
- ½ tsp of Stevia extract

Steps to Cook

1. Preheat the air fryer to 360⁰F.
2. Slice the bok choy and place it on the tray of the air fryer basket. Then sprinkle the sliced bok choy with the salt and butter.
3. Cook the bok choy for 10 minutes.
4. When the bok choy is done - let cool gently and transfer to the serving bowl.
5. Combine the chives, sesame seeds, apple cider vinegar, canola oil, and Stevia extract in the shallow bowl.
6. Add the sliced garlic and mix.
7. Then sprinkle the cooked bok choy with the prepared garlic mixture

Nutritional Information:

- Calories: 78
- Carbohydrates: 1.8g
- Fat: 7.8g
- Protein: 1g

Turnip Puree

Ingredients

- 5 turnips
- 3 oz. of butter
- ½ grated white onion
- 1 tsp salt
- 1 cup heavy cream

Steps to Cook

1. Preheat the air fryer to 400⁰F.
2. Peel the turnips and chop them.
3. Place the chopped turnips in the basket tray of the air fryer.
4. Add the butter, grated onion, salt, and heavy cream.
5. Cook the dish for 14 minutes.
6. When time is up, and turnip is cooked - let cool for 5 minutes.
7. After this, mix the turnip mixture into the puree. Use the hand blender for this step.
8. Serve the cooked turnip puree hot. Add more salt if desired.

Nutritional Information:

- Calories: 203
- Carbohydrates: 8g
- Fat: 19g
- Protein: 1.6g

Roasted Daikon

Servings: 8

Preparation time: 20 minutes

Cook time: 20 minutes

Ingredients

- 1 lb. daikon
- ½ tsp of sage
- 1 tsp salt
- 1 tbsp of olive oil
- 1 tsp dried oregano

Steps to Cook

1. Peel the daikon and cut it into cubes.
2. Sprinkle the daikon cubes with the sage, salt, and dried oregano.
3. Mix.
4. Preheat the air fryer to 360°F.
5. Place the daikon cubes on the fryer rack and sprinkle the vegetables with the olive oil.
6. Cook the daikon for 6 minutes.
7. After this, turn the daikon cubes to the other side and cook the dish for 4 more minutes.
8. When the time is up - the daikon cubes should be soft and a little golden.
9. Serve immediately.

Nutritional Information:

- Calories: 43
- Carbohydrates: 3.9g
- Fat: 2.8g
- Protein: 1.9g

Eggplant With Cheese

Servings: 7

Preparation time: 15 minutes

Cook time: 11 minutes

Ingredients

- 2 eggplant
- 1 tsp minced garlic
- 1 tsp of olive oil
- 5 oz cheddar cheese shredded
- ½ tsp of ground black pepper

Steps to Cook

1. Wash the eggplants carefully and slice them.
2. Rub the sliced aubergine with the minced garlic, salt, and ground black pepper.
3. Leave the eggplant slices for 5 minutes to marinate.
4. After this, preheat an air fryer to 400°F.
5. Place the eggplant circles in the air fryer and cook for 6 minutes.
6. Then turn the eggplant circles to the other side and cook for 5 more minutes,
7. Sprinkle the eggplant with the grated cheese and cook for another 30 seconds.

Nutritional Information:

- Calories: 127
- Carbohydrates: 9.7g
- Fat: 7.7g
- Protein: 6.6g

Sesame Okra With Egg

Servings: 4

Preparation time: 8 minutes

Cook time: 4 minutes

Ingredients

- 1 tbsp of sesame oil
- 1 tsp sesame seeds
- 11 oz. okra
- ½ tsp of salt
- 1 egg

Steps to Cook

1. Wash the okra and chop it more or less.
2. Break the egg into the bowl and beat it.
3. Add the beaten egg into the chopped okra.
4. Sprinkle with the sesame seeds and salt.
5. Preheat the air fryer to 400°F.
6. Mix the okra mixture carefully.
7. Place the okra mixture in the basket of the air fryer.
8. Sprinkle with the olive oil.
9. Cook the okra for 4 minutes.
10. When the time is up, stir the cooked dish.
11. Transfer to serving plates

Nutritional Information:

- Calories: 81
- Carbohydrates: 6.1g

- Fat: 5g
- Protein: 3g

Servings: 8

Preparation time: 7 minutes

Cook time: 10 minutes

Roasted Garlic Heads

Ingredients	Steps to Cook

Ingredients

- 1 lb. garlic heads
- 2 tbsp olive oil
- 1 tsp dried oregano
- 1 tsp dried basil
- 1 tsp ground coriander
- ¼ tsp of ground ginger

Steps to Cook

1. Cut off the ends of the garlic heads.
2. Place each head of garlic on the foil.
3. Then sprinkle the garlic heads with the olive oil, dried oregano, dried basil, ground coriander, and ground ginger.
4. Preheat the air fryer to 400°F.
5. Wrap the garlic heads in the foil and place it in the air fryer.
6. Cook the garlic heads for 10 minutes.
7. When the time is up, the garlic heads should be soft.
8. Let them cool for at least 10 minutes

Nutritional Information:

- Calories: 115
- Carbohydrates: 17.9g

- Fat: 3.8g
- Protein: 3.6g

Servings: 3

Preparation time: 10 minutes

Parmesan Cheese Sticks

Cook time: 8 minutes

Ingredients	Steps to Cook

Ingredients

- 8 oz. *parmesan*
- *1 egg*
- *½ cup of heavy cream*
- *4 tablespoons of almond flour*
- *¼ tsp of ground black pepper*

Steps to Cook

1. Beat the egg in the bowl and beat it.
2. Add the heavy cream and the almond flour.
3. Next, sprinkle the mixture with the ground black pepper.
4. Mix gently or use the hand mixer.
5. After this, cut the cheese into the short thick sticks.
6. Dip the cheese sticks in the heavy cream mixture.
7. Next, place the cheese sticks in the plastic bags and freeze them.
8. Preheat the air fryer to 400°F.
9. Place the cheese sticks on the fryer shelf.
10. Cook the cheese sticks for 8 minutes.

Nutritional Information:

- Calories: 389
- Carbohydrates: 5.5g

- Fat: 29.5g
- Protein: 28.6g

Snow Peas Puree

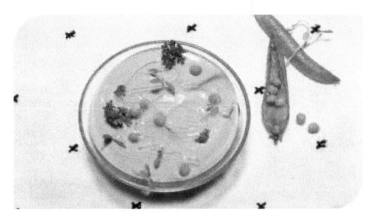

Ingredients	Steps to Cook

Ingredients

- ½ a cup of heavy cream
- 1 tsp of butter
- 1 tsp salt
- 1 tsp of paprika
- 1 lb. snow peas
- ¼ tsp of nutmeg

Steps to Cook

1. Preheat the air fryer to 400°F.
2. Wash the snow peas carefully and place them in the air fryer basket tray.
3. Then sprinkle the snow peas with the butter, salt, paprika, nutmeg, and heavy cream.
4. Cook the snow peas for 5 minutes.
5. When the time is up, gently shake the snow peas and transfer to serving plates.

Nutritional Information:

- Calories: 110
- Carbohydrates: 8.8g
- Fat: 6.9g
- Protein: 4.1g

Fennel Wedges

Servings: 5

Preparation time: 15 minutes

Cook time: 6 minutes

Ingredients	Steps to Cook

Ingredients

- 1 tsp of Stevia extract
- ½ tsp of fresh thyme
- ½ tsp of salt
- 1 tsp canola oil
- 14 oz. fennel
- 1 tsp of butter
- 1 tsp dried oregano
- ½ tsp of chili flakes

Steps to Cook

1. Cut the fennel into wedges.
2. Melt the butter.
3. Combine the butter, canola oil, dried oregano, and chili flakes in the bowl.
4. Coat the mixture.
5. Add salt, fresh thyme, and Stevia extract.
6. Whisk gently.
7. Next, brush the fennel wedges with the rotated mixture.
8. Preheat the air fryer to 370⁰F.
9. Place the fennel wedges on the fryer rack.
10. Cook the fennel wedges for 3 minutes on each side.

Nutritional Information:

- Calories: 41
- Carbohydrates: 6.1g
- Fat: 1.9g
- Protein: 1g

Kohlrabi Fritters

Servings: 5

Preparation time: 10 minutes

Cook time: 7 minutes

Ingredients	Steps to Cook
<ul><li>8 oz kohlrabi</li><li>1 egg</li><li>1 tbsp of almond flour</li><li>½ tsp of salt</li><li>1 tsp of olive oil</li><li>1 tsp ground black pepper</li><li>1 tbsp dried parsley</li><li>¼ tsp of chili.</li></ul>	1. Peel the kohlrabi and grate it. 2. Combine the grated kohlrabi with the salt, ground black pepper, dried parsley, and chili. 3. Beat the egg into the mixture and beat it. 4. After this, make the medium fritters from the mixture. 5. Preheat the air fryer to 380^{0}F. 6. Spray the basket tray of the air fryer with the olive oil inside and place the fritters there. 7. Cook the fritters for 4 minutes. 8. After this, turn the fritters to the other side and cook for 3 more minutes.

Nutritional Information:

- Calories: 66
- Carbohydrates: 4.4g

- Fat: 4.7g
- Protein: 3.2g

Delicious Bamboo Shoots

Servings: 2

Preparation time: 8 minutes

Cook time: 4 minutes

Ingredients

- 8 oz. bamboo shoots
- 2 garlic cloves, sliced
- 1 tbsp of olive oil
- ½ tsp of chili flakes
- 2 tbsp chives
- ½ tsp of salt
- 3 tbsp of fish broth

Steps to Cook

1. Preheat the air fryer to 400⁰F.
2. Cut the bamboo shoots into strips.
3. Combine the sliced garlic cloves, olive oil, chili flakes, salt, and fish broth in the air fryer basket tray.
4. Cook for 1 minute.
5. After this, gently stir the mixture.
6. Add the strips of bamboo shoots and chives.
7. Stir the dish carefully and cook for 3 more minutes.
8. Next, stir the cooked garnish carefully.
9. Transfer it to the service plates.

Nutritional Information:

- Calories: 100
- Carbohydrates: 7g
- Fat: 7.4g
- Protein: 3.7g

Servings: 4

Preparation time: 15 minutes

Cook time: 15 minutes

Summer Vegetables

Ingredients	Steps to Cook

Ingredients

- 1 eggplant
- 1 tomato
- 1 zucchini
- 1 white onion
- 2 green peppers
- 1 tsp of paprika
- 1 tbsp canola oil
- ½ tsp of ground nutmeg
- ½ tsp of ground thyme
- 1 tsp salt

Steps to Cook

1. Preheat the air fryer to 390°F.
2. Carefully wash the eggplant, tomato, and zucchini.
3. Peel the onion. Chop up all the prepared vegetables more or less. Next, place the chopped vegetables in the basket tray of the air fryer.
4. Sprinkle the vegetables with the paprika, canola oil, ground nutmeg, ground thyme, and salt.
5. Stir the vegetables carefully with the help of two spatulas.
6. Cut the green peppers into squares. Next, add the pepper squares to the vegetable mixture. Stir gently.
7. Cook the dish for 15 minutes. Stir the vegetables after 10 minutes carefully

Nutritional Information:

- Calories: 96
- Carbohydrates: 14.8g
- Fat: 4.1g
- Protein: 2.4g

Chapter 6

Dinner Recipes

Zucchini Chips

Servings: 5

Preparation time: 8 minutes

Cook time: 13 minutes

Ingredients	Steps to Cook

Ingredients

- 2 zucchini
- 1 tsp of olive oil
- ½ tsp of salt
- 1 tsp of paprika

Steps to Cook

1. Wash the zucchini carefully and cut it into chips.
2. Preheat the air fryer to 370°F.
3. Sprinkle the zucchini slices with the salt and paprika. After this, place the zucchini slices in the air fryer. Gently spread the zucchini slices with the olive oil— Cook the zucchini strips for 13 minutes.
4. Turn the zucchini strips to another side during cooking if desired. When the zucchini fries are cooked, let them cool well.

Nutritional Information:

- Calories: 22
- Carbohydrates: 2.9g

- Fat: 1.1g
- Protein: 1g

Radish Chips

Servings: 12

Preparation time: 8 minutes

Cook time: 15 minutes

Ingredients

- 1 lb. radish
- 2 tbsp olive oil
- 1 tsp salt

Steps to Cook

1. Wash the radish carefully and cut it to the size of the chips.
2. After this, sprinkle the radish shavings with the salt.
3. Drizzle the radish shavings with the olive oil.
4. Preheat the air fryer to 375°F.
5. Place the radish slices in the air fryer and cook the chips for 15 minutes.
6. When the radish shavings get the desired texture, they are cooked.
7. Chill the chips and serve.

Nutritional Information:

- Calories: 26
- Carbohydrates: 1.3g
- Fat: 2.4g
- Protein: 0.3g

Squid Rings

Servings: 4

Preparation time: 12 minutes

Cook time: 8 minutes

Ingredients	Steps to Cook

Ingredients

- 1 cup of almond flour
- 9 oz. squid
- 1 egg
- ½ tsp of lemon zest
- 1 tsp fresh lemon juice
- ½ tsp of turmeric
- ¼ tsp of salt
- ¼ tsp of ground black pepper

Steps to Cook

1. Wash and peel the squid. Then cut the squid into thick rings. Beat the egg in the bowl and beat it.
2. Sprinkle the beaten egg with the lemon zest, turmeric, salt, and ground black pepper.
3. Sprinkle the squid rings with the fresh lemon juice.
4. After this, put the squid rings in the beaten egg and stir carefully.
5. Leave the squid rings in the egg mixture for 4 minutes. Next, coat the squid rings well in the almond flour mixture.
6. Preheat the air fryer to 360°F.
7. Transfer the calamari rings to the fryer rack.
8. Cook the squid rings for 8 minutes.

Nutritional Information:

- Calories: 190
- Carbohydrates: 7g
- Fat: 15.7g
- Protein: 8.7g

Roasted Almond

Ingredients

- ¼ cup of hazelnuts
- ¼ cup of walnuts
- ½ a cup of walnuts
- ½ a cup of macadamia nuts
- 1 tbsp of olive oil
- 1 tsp salt

Steps to Cook

1. Preheat the air fryer to 320 degrees Fahrenheit.
2. Place the hazelnuts, walnuts, walnuts, and macadamia nuts in the air fryer.
3. Cook the walnuts for 8 minutes.
4. Stir the walnuts after 4 minutes of cooking.
5. At the end of cooking, sprinkle the nuts with the olive oil and salt and shake well.
6. Cook the walnuts for 1 more minute.
7. Then transfer the cooked walnuts into the serving ramekins.

Nutritional Information:

- Calories: 230
- Carbohydrates: 3.9g
- Fat: 23.9g
- Protein: 3.9g

Almond Butter Bread

Servings: 22

Preparation time: 30 minutes

Cook time: 30 minutes

Ingredients	Steps to Cook
<ul><li>6 eggs</li><li>5 oz. almond flour</li><li>4 tbsp butter, melted</li><li>3 tsp baking powder</li><li>1 lemon wedge</li><li>1 tsp salt</li><li>6 drops liquid stevia</li></ul>	1. Preheat the air fryer to 375°F. 2. Separate the yolks from the whites. Beat the egg whites to the point of snow. When they start to rise, add 3 drops of lemon. Keep beating until "peaks" and is like a meringue. 3. In a separate bowl, add the yolks, melted butter, almond flour, baking powder, and salt. Mix everything well; a compact mass will remain. 4. To this mixture, add 1/3 of the egg whites and mix with enveloping movements. Keep adding the whites little by little, always wrapping them. 5. You will get a fluffy dough. Grease the mold with a little butter and pour the batter. 6. Bake 30 minutes at 375°F. 7. After 30 minutes, insert a needle or knife into the bread: if it comes out clean, that's it. If not, leave it in the oven for a few more minutes. 8. Let cool 30 minutes before unmolding. Unmold the bread and leave to cool on a rack for another 30 minutes. Cut it into slices and enjoy!

Nutritional Information:

- Calories: 184.2
- Carbohydrates: 4.6g
- Fat: 15.8g
- Protein: 8.9g

Lemon Coconut Pudding

Servings: 5

Preparation time: 8 minutes

Cook time: 25 minutes

Ingredients

- 3 ½ oz. grated coconut
- ½ cup of sugar
- ½ lb. self-rising flour
- 1 lemon (juice and zest)
- 2 tbsp cornstarch
- 1 egg
- 1 tsp vanilla essence
- ¼ cup sunflower oil

Steps to Cook

1. Preheat the air fryer to 360°F.
2. Beat the egg with the sugar, then add the lemon juice and oil.
3. Add the lemon zest and vanilla essence.
4. Mix the dry ingredients and add them to the preparation.
5. Place the mixture in a buttered and floured pan.
6. Bake in the preheated air fryer for 25 minutes or until a toothpick sticks in it comes out dry.

Nutritional Information:

- Calories: 167.2
- Carbohydrates: 16.3g
- Fat: 13.8g
- Protein: 3.2g

Roasted Avocados With Mozzarella

Servings: 2

Preparation time: 5 minutes

Cook time: 15 minutes

Ingredients

- 1 avocado
- Lemon juice
- ½ tomato
- 1 oz. Mozzarella cheese
- ½ tsp Salt flakes pinch
- 2 tsp Extra virgin olive oil
- 8 Fresh oregano (leaves)

Steps to Cook

1. Cut the avocado in half lengthwise, carefully remove the seed, and brush each half with lemon juice. Cut the meat of the avocado halves making a rhomboid pattern and deep cuts that come to the base.
2. Drain the mozzarella and cut two pieces the same size as the cavities of the avocados. Fill them with the cheese.
3. Put them in the preheated air fryer to 360°F with heat up and down, for 15 minutes or until the mozzarella has melted well.
4. Meanwhile, wash the tomato and cut one of its halves into small dice. When the avocado is ready, remove it from the oven and place the tomato cubes on the surface. Sprinkle salt flakes, fresh oregano leaves, and drizzle with extra virgin olive oil before serving.

Nutritional Information:

- Calories: 220
- Carbohydrates: 9g

- Fat: 18g
- Protein: 7g

Mini Muffins With Blueberries

Servings: 8

Preparation time: 10 minutes

Cook time: 12 minutes

Ingredients

- 2 Eggs
- 60 ml Milk or vegetable alternative
- ½ lb. ground almonds
- 1 tsp Vanilla essence
- 1 tsp yeast
- A pinch of Salt
- Sweetener suitable for liquid cooking, equivalent to about 2 oz. g of sugar (optional)
- Fresh blueberries
- Chia seeds (optional)

Steps to Cook

1. Preheat the air fryer to 360°F and prepare a tray with suitable molds.
2. In a bowl, beat the eggs, milk, and vanilla essence with a whisk. Reserve.
3. Mix the almond flour with the yeast and salt, and form a hole. Pour in the liquid dough, add the sweetener if using and combine gently.
4. When the dough is homogeneous, distribute it into the molds without filling them to the top. Introduce 3-4 fresh blueberries previously washed and dried, pressing gently, and add some chia seeds on top, if desired.
5. Bake for about 10-12 minutes or until they have risen and are firm to the touch, slightly golden. Wait for a little out of the air fryer before unmolding.

Nutritional Information:

- Calories: 218
- Carbohydrates: 6.1g
- Fat: 19.3g
- Protein: 6.9g

Eggplant Chips

Servings: 2

Preparation time: 5 minutes

Cook time: 15 minutes

Ingredients	Steps to Cook

Ingredients

- ½ eggplant
- ½ cup almond flour
- ¼ tsp. Cayenne pepper
- salt and pepper
- ½ egg
- ½ tbsp. coconut oil in spray form

Steps to Cook

1. Preheat the air fryer to 400°F.
2. Peel the eggplant and cut into the shape of French fries. Sprinkle a little salt on all sides. Reserve.
3. In a shallow bowl, mix the ground almonds, cayenne pepper, salt, and black pepper. Break the eggs into another bowl and beat until foamy.
4. Dip the pieces of eggplants in the ground almond mixture, then in the beaten eggs, and then again in the almond mixture.
5. After bathing, place the eggplant "potatoes" on a greased baking sheet and drizzle melted coconut oil on top.
6. Bake for 15 minutes or until crisp and golden.

Nutritional Information:

- Calories: 257
- Carbohydrates: 5g
- Fat: 21g
- Protein: 8g

Chocolate Muffins

Servings: 6
Preparation time: 10 minutes
Cook time: 15 minutes

Ingredients	Steps to Cook

Ingredients

- 1 ½ oz. granulated sugar
- ½ cup coconut milk or soy milk
- 1/3 cup coconut oil, liquid
- 1 tsp of vanilla extract
- 4 oz. all-purpose flour
- 3 tsp cocoa powder
- 1 tsp baking powder
- ½ tsp of baking soda
- a pinch of salt
- 3 oz. of chocolate chips
- 1 oz. pistachios, cracked (optional)
- Non-stick spray oil

Steps to Cook

1. Put the sugar, coconut milk, coconut oil, and vanilla extract in a small bowl. Set aside.
2. Mix the flour, cocoa powder, baking powder, baking soda, and salt in a separate bowl and set aside.
3. Mix the dry ingredients with the wet ingredients gradually, until smooth. Then mix with the chocolate and pistachio.
4. Select Preheat, in the air fryer, adjust the temperature to 300^{0}F.
5. Grease the muffin tins with cooking spray and pour the mixture until they are full to ¾.
6. Carefully place the muffin tins in the preheated air fryer. Select Desserts set the time to 15 minutes.
7. Remove the muffins when the cooking is done and let them cool for 10 minutes before serving.

Nutritional Information:

- Calories: 690
- Carbohydrates: 79.2g
- Fat: 38g
- Protein: 9.9g

Sweet Sponge Cake

Servings: 10
Preparation time: 10 min
Cook time: 50 minutes

Ingredients	Steps to Cook

Ingredients

- ½ lb. flour for
- yeast pastry
- ½ lb. of sugar
- 3 medium eggs
- 3 tbsp olive oil
- Orange zest
- ¾ lb. chopped pistachio
- 1 envelope of yeast

Steps to Cook

1. Separate the yolks from the eggs. Mount the egg whites until stiff with the mixer and gradually incorporate the sugar.
2. Mix until you get a thick white cream.
3. Separately, beat the yolks with the oil and the orange zest. Incorporate this mixture with the whites, mix in an enveloping way, and finally incorporate the flour and yeast with a sieve. When everything is well mixed, add the pistachios. You can use a circular mold greased with oil and flour or kitchen paper that is more comfortable. Add the cake batter to the pan.
4. Preheat the air fryer for a few minutes at 320⁰F. Put the mold in the basket of the Air fryer and program the timer for about 30 minutes at 320⁰F temperature.
5. While it is cooking, prepare the lemon cream.
6. To do this, gradually mix the white with the sugar, add the lemon juice and add the sour cream and mix until obtaining a thick cream and ready.

Nutritional Information:

- Calories: 110
- Carbohydrates: 23g
- Fat: 1g
- Protein: 2.1g

Egg Custard

Servings: 4
Preparation time: 10 minutes
Cook time: 60 minutes

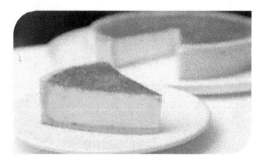

Ingredients	Steps to Cook

Ingredients

- 1 ¼ cup milk
- 3 eggs
- 3 oz. of sugar

Steps to Cook

1. Put the sugar in a saucepan, reserving two tablespoons for later. Add a little water. With very low heat, melt the sugar until it is all liquid and caramelized.
2. Immediately pour into the pudding molds. It is essential to do it right away because the caramel solidifies very quickly on cooling.
3. In a separate bowl, beat the eggs with the help of some rods. When they start frothing, add the milk and mix everything very well.
4. Once the mixture is homogeneous, pour into the molds you will have previously put the caramel.
5. Then preheat the Air fryer for a few minutes to 360°F.
6. Then cook the custards in a bain-marie in the Air fryer. To do this, arrange the custards inside the basket of the Air fryer in a container with water ensuring that the water reaches half of the containers but ensuring that no water enters them.
7. Put the container with the flan and the medium water bathing them in the air fryer and cook everything at medium temperature 320°F for about 1 hour.
8. To check if the flans are cooked, shake gently, and if they have the consistent appearance of the flans when they are moved, they are ready. Otherwise, if they look very liquid, bake them in a bain-marie a little more.

Nutritional Information:

- Calories: 146.6
- Carbohydrates: 15.5g
- Fat: 6.5g
- Protein: 7.1g

Cheddar Cheese Bites

Servings: 8
Preparation time: 1 minute
Cook time: 20 minutes

Ingredients

- 1 8 squares of cheddar cheese
- Mashed potatoes
- Flour
- Egg and breadcrumbs
- Extra virgin olive oil

Steps to Cook

1. Make the mashed potatoes as you like.
2. Cut the cheddar cheese into small squares.
3. Take a piece of cheese and wrap it with a thin layer of mashed potatoes.
4. When you have the 8 pieces wrapped in the mashed potatoes, take it to the freezer for about 30 minutes.
5. Go through the flour and shake.
6. Go through the beaten egg, breadcrumbs, again through the beaten egg and through the breadcrumbs.
7. Take to the refrigerator at least 30 minutes.
8. Place in the basket of the Air fryer and paint well with extra virgin olive oil.
9. Select 20 minutes at 360°F.

Nutritional Information:

- Calories: 130
- Carbohydrates: 20g
- Fat: 3.5g
- Protein: 3g

Mini Potato And Egg Pizza

Servings: 6-8
Preparation time: 10 min
Cook time: 35 minutes

Ingredients	Steps to Cook

Ingredients

- ½ lb. of wheat flour
- ¼ lb. of water
- 5 tsp of extra virgin olive oil
- 2 tsp of salt
- 2 tsp of yeast
- 8 eggs
- 2 potatoes
- extra virgin olive oil
- Salt
- Ketchup
- Oregano
- Bacon
- Grated cheese

Steps to Cook

1. Peel the potatoes and cut them into a long, thick stick. Put salt, a little oil, and mix.
2. Put them in the pan of the Air fryer and select 30 minutes. Reserve.
3. Continue with the pizza dough. For this, put in the food processor with a kneading hook, the flour, water, oil, salt, and yeast. Knead at low speed for at least 5 minutes. Make a ball and let it rest for 30 minutes. Divide the dumpling into 8 equal parts.
4. Spread the masses. Put a small layer of tomato sauce and sprinkle with oregano. Place the potatoes on the edge of the pizza dough. Press a little so that they are well fixed in the dough. Take to the preheated air fryer, 360⁰F, 15 minutes.
5. Remove the mini pizza slices and add a layer of chopped bacon and on the bacon, crack an egg in each mini pizza. Cover with grated cheese on the part of the white, leaving the yolk in sight. Return to the air fryer, 360⁰F, another 10 to 20 minutes.

Nutritional Information:

- Calories: 179.7
- Carbohydrates: 34.2g
- Fat: 3.3g

- Protein: 5.2g
- Sugar: 0.6g
- Cholesterol: 0mg

Chocolate And Walnut Cake

Servings: 2-4

Preparation time: 5 minutes

Cook time: 20 minutes

Ingredients	Steps to Cook

Ingredients

- 2 ¼ oz dark chocolate
- 2 butter spoons
- 1 egg
- 3 tbsp of sugar
- 2 oz. flour
- 1 envelope Royal yeast
- Chopped walnuts

Steps to Cook

1. Melt the dark chocolate with the butter over low heat. Once melted, put in a bowl.
2. Incorporate the egg, sugar, flour, yeast, and finally, the chopped nuts.
3. Beat well by hand until a uniform dough is obtained.
4. Put the dough in a silicone mold or oven suitable for incorporation in the basket of the Air fryer.
5. Preheat the air fryer for a few minutes at 1800C.
6. Set the timer for 20 minutes at 1800C and when it has cooled, remove from the mold.

Nutritional Information:

- Calories: 310
- Carbohydrates: 44g
- Fat: 14g
- Protein: 5g

Light Cheese Cake

Servings: 8
Preparation time: 5 minutes
Cook time: 55 minutes

Ingredients

- 1 lb. of cottage cheese
- 3 whole eggs
- 2 tbsp of sweetener powder
- 2 tbsp of oat bran
- ½ tbsp of baking yeast
- 2 tbsp of cinnamon
- 2 tbsp vanilla flavoring
- 1 lemon (the skin)

Steps to Cook

1. Mix the cottage cheese, the sweetener, the cinnamon, the vanilla flavor, and the lemon zest in a bowl. Mix very well until you get a homogeneous cream.
2. Incorporate the eggs one by one.
3. Finally, add the oats and yeast, mixing well.
4. Put all the mixture in a container so that it fits in the Air fryer.
5. Preheat the air fryer for a few minutes at 360°F.
6. Put the mold in the basket of the Air fryer and adjust the timer for about 20 minutes at 360°F.

Nutritional Information:

- Calories: 222
- Carbohydrates: 9g
- Fat: 14g
- Protein: 18g

Blackberry Pie With Cheese

Servings: 4
Preparation time: 5 minutes
Cook time: 20-30 minutes

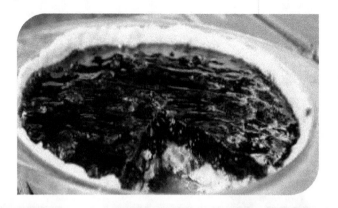

Ingredients

- 2 cups blackberry
- 1 cup of sugar
- 1 tbsp of lemon juice
- enough flour to spread
- ½ lb. of puff pastry
- ½ cups cream cheese, diced
- enough egg, to varnish
- enough of icing sugar to decorate

Steps to Cook

1. Preheat the air fryer to 400°F.
2. In a saucepan, cook the blackberries with the sugar for about 30 minutes over low heat or until it has a thick consistency, add the lemon juice and mix well. Let cool and reserve.
3. On a floured surface, spread the puff pastry approximately 3 mm thick and with the help of a 10 cm diameter round cutter, cut discs.
4. Fill the puff pastry discs with the blackberry jam and cream cheese, close and with your hands, make a fold, place on a tray, and garnish with egg.
5. Put in the air fryer for 20 minutes or until golden, let cool and decorate with icing sugar.

Nutritional Information:

- Calories: 470
- Carbohydrates: 57 g
- Fat: 27g
- Protein: 6g

Apple Pie And Sweet Milk

Servings: 6-8
Preparation time: 5 minutes
Cook time: 20 minutes

Ingredients	Steps to Cook

Ingredients

- 3 apples
- 1/3 cups cranberry
- ½ cups of walnut
- ½ cups of rum
- enough flour to spread
- ½ lb. of puff pastry
- ¾ cups of sweet milk
- 1 egg, to varnish
- enough walnut, finely chopped, to decorate

Steps to Cook

1. Preheat the air fryer to 400⁰F.
2. For the filling, peel and cut the apples into very thin sheets, place in a bowl and mix with the walnuts, blueberries, and rum. Macerate for 30 minutes, drain very well, and reserve.
3. Spread the puff pastry on a floured surface 3 mm thick, with a 10 cm diameter cutter that cuts discs.
4. Fill the puff pastry discs with the apples and a little sweet milk, with your hands, make folds to close the empanadas. Place on a tray, garnish with egg, and sprinkle with walnuts.
5. Put in the air fryer for 20 minutes or until golden. Serve with milk or coffee.

Nutritional Information:

- Calories: 750
- Carbohydrates: 82g

- Fat: 37g
- Protein: 15g

Lemon Cake

Servings: 6
Preparation time: 5 minutes
Cook time: 30 minutes

Ingredients

- ¼ lb. all-purpose flour
- 1 tsp baking powder
- a pinch of salt
- 3 oz. unsalted butter, softened
- ¼ lb. granulated sugar
- 1 large egg
- ½ oz. of fresh lemon juice
- 1 lemon, lemon zest
- 2 oz. of whey

Steps to Cook

1. Mix the flour, baking powder, and salt in a bowl. Set aside. Add the softened butter to an electric mixer and beat until smooth and fluffy—a—approximately 3 minutes. Beat the sugar in the butter for 1 minute.
2. Whisk the flour mixture in the butter until entirely united, for about 1 minute. Add the egg, lemon juice, and lemon zest. Mix until everything is completely united. Slowly pour in the buttermilk while mixing on medium speed.
3. Add the mixture to a greased mini-loaf pan on top.
4. Select Preheat; in the air fryer. Adjust the temperature to 320°F. Place the cake in the preheated air fryer. Select Pan set the time to 30 minutes.

Nutritional Information:

- Calories: 326
- Carbohydrates: 12.1g
- Fat: 25.2g
- Protein: 13.4g

Healthy Carrot Chips

Servings: 3
Preparation time: 5 min
Cook time: 20-25 minutes

Ingredients

- carrots to taste
- 2 tablespoons extra virgin olive oil
- salt to taste

Steps to Cook

1. Wash the carrots very well and remove the ends.
2. Cut the carrots into very thin slices, either using a mandolin or with a food processor.
3. Add the oil and, with clean hands, spread it over all the carrots. Put the carrot slices in the basket of your air fryer and program it at 330°F for 20-25 minutes, depending on the number of carrots you make.
4. Every 5-7 minutes, open the basket and shake it vigorously so that they are removed, and put the basket back inside to continue to be made. Watch from the 15th minute that they do not burn, since it depends on the amount you do can be done before. Take out the carrots, put some salt on them, and ready.

Nutritional Information:

- Calories: 35
- Carbohydrates: 8g
- Fat: 2g
- Protein: 1g

Focaccia

Servings: 4
Preparation time: 45 minu
Cook time: 20 minutes

Ingredients	Steps to Cook

Ingredients

- ½ oz. dry yeast
- ½ cup of warm water
- 1 cup baker's flour

Mass:

- ½ oz. dry yeast
- ½ pound baker's flour
- Warm water

Steps to Cook

1. Assemble the sponge for 40 minutes. Assemble the dough, unite with the sponge for 45 minutes, knead degassing until the dough joins, and becomes smooth.

2. Assemble the pastries, they can roll 1 ½ tbsp loaves, or in a source place the extended dough, let it take half an hour. In the extended dough, drip olive oil, rosemary, tomatoes, onion into slices, and bake at 360^0F 10 minutes approximately both bread and focaccia.

Nutritional Information:

- Calories: 387.9
- Carbohydrates: 64.4g
- Fat: 9.9g
- Protein: 9g

Chocolate Cake

Servings: 2
Preparation time: 5 minutes
Cook time: 40 minutes

Ingredients

- 2 eggs
- 1 homemade chocolate soy yogurt
- 1 container of yogurt sugar
- 2 containers of sponge cake flour
- ½ container of oil
- ½ sachet baking powder
- Orange zest

Steps to Cook

1. Preheat deep fryer to 250⁰F for 5 minutes.
2. In a bowl, put the eggs, the yogurt, and sugar, beat and then add the flour, the yeast, the oil, and the orange zest.
3. Mix all.
4. In the bucket of the fryer, mold on purpose for the fryer but also a mold that burns inside. Put the oven paper down the mold and add the dough.
5. Put in a fryer Cupcakes program 15 minutes at 300⁰F. Then make some crosscuts on the cake and put another 15 minutes with the same temperature. If it is not cooked inside, add about 5 minutes more at 280⁰F.

Nutritional Information:

- Calories: 424
- Carbohydrates: 58g
- Fat: 22g
- Protein: 3.8g

Roasted Pears

Servings: 4
Preparation time: 10 minutes
Cook time: 20 minutes

Ingredients	Steps to Cook

Ingredients

- 4 pears in shell, well washed
- ¼ cup of raisins
- 2 tbsp sugar-free jam, the one you like the most
- 1 tsp honey
- 1 pinch cinnamon powder

Steps to Cook

1. Wash the pears, hollowed out by removing the core.
2. Separate the pulp.
3. Mix the chosen jam with the pulp of the pears, honey, and raisins, and cinnamon.
4. Fill the pears with that mixture.
5. Place the pears in the fryer.
6. In the container, place a glass of water.
7. Cook for 20 minutes at 360^0F.
8. Serve them alone or accompanied with a scoop of vanilla ice cream.

Nutritional Information:

- Calories: 84
- Carbohydrates: 22g
- Fat: 1g
- Protein: 1g

Tatin Mini Cake

Servings: 6
Preparation time: 10 minutes
Cook time: 30 minutes

Ingredients	Steps to Cook
<ul><li>3 ½ oz. flour</li><li>1 ½ oz. cold butter</li><li>5 tsp water</li><li>1 pinch of salt</li><li>1 apple</li><li>Lemon juice</li><li>1 oz. Sugar</li><li>½ oz. butter</li></ul>	1. Put the salt in the flour and the cold butter. Mix everything until it is like sand. Add the 5 tsp of water and mix it until obtaining a homogeneous mass. Wrap it in transparent paper and reserve. In a clay pot, put the sugar and butter and let it melt and toast. Peel the apple, use the lemon juice to spread it. When your sugar and butter are already browned, put the apples on top, and place them tightly, cover the entire surface very well. Leave the apples caramelizing for 15 to 20 minutes; control them. 2. While stretch the dough. You can do it as you find it more manageable. Once the apples are caramelized, top with the short-crust pastry. Cut what is left and adjust to the contour. 3. Preheat the fryer to 220°F, and put the cake for about 15 minutes.

Nutritional Information:

- Calories: 355.7
- Carbohydrates: 62.9g
- Fat: 12.3g
- Protein: 2.1g

Gluten-Free Yogurt Cupcake

Servings: 3
Preparation time: 3 minutes
Cook time: 40 minutes

Ingredients	Steps to Cook

Ingredients

- 1 Greek yogurt
- 3 eggs
- 4 ½ oz. sugar
- 3 oz. cream
- 1 ½ oz. sunflower oil
- 1 ½ oz. butter
- 6 oz. gluten-free flour
- Salt
- 1 sachet yeast

Steps to Cook

1. Put the eggs, yogurt, and sugar in the air fryer. Mix well. Add the rest of the ingredients and mix.
2. Put the dough in the cake container, previously brushed with oil. Preheat the fryer and put the mold with the dough for 40 minutes at 240°F.
3. When it cools, we unmold and decorate to taste.

Nutritional Information:

- Calories: 131
- Carbohydrates: 16g
- Fat: 6.3g
- Protein: 2.4g

Rabas

Servings: 2
Preparation time: 5 minutes
Cook time: 10 minutes

Ingredients	Steps to Cook
• 16 rabas • 1 egg • Bread crumbs • Condiments: salt, pepper, sweet paprika	1. If they are frozen put them in hot water and they boil for 2 minutes. 2. Remove and dry well. 3. Beat the egg and season to taste, salt, pepper and sweet paprika. Place in the egg. 4. Bread with breadcrumbs. Place on sticks. 5. Place in the fryer for 5 minutes at 320^0F. Remove 6. Sprinkle with fritolin and place 5 more minutes at 400^0F.

Nutritional Information:

- Calories: 200
- Carbohydrates: 1g

- Fat: 1g
- Protein: 1g

Conclusion

In this eBook, we have seen a lot about an air fryer. As we have seen in chapter 1; the concept of air fryer; which is simply a revolutionary kitchen appliance for cooking food through the circulation of superheated air. They're also significant advantages using this appliance. For this reason, we gave you some tips so that you can take advantage of using it.

Oil-free fryers are all the rage in the kitchen. It is a simple but innovative cooking method. You can cook any type of food that would otherwise get soaked in deep fat.

So, you have just seen in the preceding chapters, a great variety of recipes that you can take advantage of with your air fryer. Don't let time kill you by working on cooking traditionally. Take advantage of your time, health, and, above all, the flavor cooking with an air fryer.

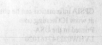

CPSIA information can be obtained
at www.ICGtesting.com
Printed in the USA
LVHW02234716I020
668889LV00017B/503